CRYPTOCURRENCY TRADING

Beginner's Guide to Technical Trading Bitcoin and Cryptocurrencies

By

TROY HEARTH

COPYRIGHT & DISCLOSURES

TABLE OF CONTENTS

CHAPTER 1
Foreword

Are you new to the cryptocurrency market and wondering how to make money through Bitcoin trading? Don't worry, this tutorial will teach you step-by-step how to trade Bitcoin and can be applied to other cryptocurrencies as well. Bitcoin Trading is a comprehensive and beginner-friendly guide for those who want to venture into cryptocurrency trading. This tutorial will teach readers how to read charts and determine when to buy or sell by using technical analysis tools. Readers will also know which strategies to use to boost their Bitcoin profits and how to take advantage of Bull and Bear markets.

This guide will teach you how to take profits and control your size and position in the market in addition to seeing when to stop trading to minimize losses. This guide will teach you how to read technical charts, draw support and resistance levels, and determine entry and exit points.

You will also learn to determine whether a crypto asset is overbought or oversold using oscillator tools. Using the strength of price momentum, you will learn how to pinpoint the specific points to make buy and sell orders.

By knowing how to analyze trading charts, potential investors will see not only how to determine entry and exit points but also analyze market trends, identify price directions, and ascertain price reversal points in a trend.

Readers will also discover usable strategies to make Bitcoin money, boost their returns, and take price action decisions. They will also learn about automated trading bots and exchange platforms through which they can trade their Bitcoins.

The cryptocurrency market is highly volatile and associated with different types of risks. This tutorial educates readers on different types of Bitcoin risks and offers the tactics and mindsets needed to manage them. It also includes specific risk-response strategies readers can use to manage market risks. Traders will also know how to use stop-loss orders to limit losses when prices drop. With stop-loss orders, traders don't have to monitor price movement daily, a convenient perk if traveling or indisposed when the price moves against their trade.

IF YOU PLAN TO VENTURE INTO BITCOIN TRADING OR ANY OTHER CRYPTOCURRENCY INVESTMENT, THIS GUIDE WILL PROVIDE YOU WITH ALL THE TOOLS AND SECRETS YOU NEED FOR SUCCESSFUL AND FINANCIALLY REWARDING TRADING.

CHAPTER 2
Overview of Cryptocurrency

Intro

A cryptocurrency is a decentralized digital asset that acts as a medium for currency exchange by using cryptography to secure transactions and verify asset transfers.

Whew, that's a mouthful, let's break it down:

• Decentralized: Relies upon a community (no central bank, person, etc)

• Medium for Currency Exchange: A way to buy and sell

• Cryptographic concept to secure transactions and verify asset transfers: The buy and sell transactions are locked by the buyer and seller but the decentralized community can verify that the transaction is valid.

Similar to stock exchanges, cryptocurrency is typically traded over the internet via a cryptocurrency exchange. You can transfer any cryptocurrency to someone in exchange for fiat currency (cash) but how do you find those buyers and sellers? The cryptocurrency exchange matches buyers to sellers to make it more convenient. Surprisingly, in this case, the exchange is centralized for convenience but it is worth it to have the legitimacy of an exchange and the large pool of buyers and sellers when converting money.

Bitcoin (BTC) is one of the most commonly traded cryptocurrencies. Cryptocurrencies are transferred between peers without middleman involvement or central government control. As with normal currencies, you can obtain a cryptocurrency by either exchanging goods or services or trading your dollars. Alternatively, you can trade a cryptocurrency with another cryptocurrency. The price of each cryptocurrency asset is set based on supply and demand.

Anyone can trade dollars for cryptocurrencies with third parties like brokers and exchanges. Cryptocurrency prices are highly volatile so expect the value of the cryptocurrency to fluctuate.

The majority of traders prefer using Bitcoin due to its popularity. As a bonus, no one controls or owns its network. Due to its low transaction fees and global power, many traders use Bitcoin for all their financial transactions.

Once a trading transaction takes place, it cannot be altered. This has both good and bad sides since there is no method of resolving disputes like a credit card charge-back.

Bitcoin has yielded high returns for early adopters and continues to be adopted by more merchants every year. It is more than ten years old and its adoption continues to increase, making it stronger and more secure.

Bitcoin and other cryptocurrency prices (also called altcoins) can be viewed in chart form on TradingView, which provides real-time data on the cryptocurrency market.

Cryptocurrency Charting Using TradingView

TradingView is a platform that provides trading information

to investors and traders. Beginners and long-term investors can receive real-time information and trending news concerning their preferred cryptocurrency. TradingView generates the charts used throughout this book. TradingView is free to use but periodic ads will be displayed.

Cycle of Human Emotions

Emotions present a huge stumbling block to an investment's success. Emotions can affect your investment decisions. For example, when chasing crypto-asset performance, you can enter or exit the market immediately to avoid risks. These emotions will limit you from reaching long-term financial goals.

As a trader, you need to learn to minimize these emotions while trading. Doing so requires a lot of practice and restraint to avoid emotional trading. Most traders experience emotional cycles like hope, greed, euphoria, anxiety, denial, despair, and hope again while making trading decisions.

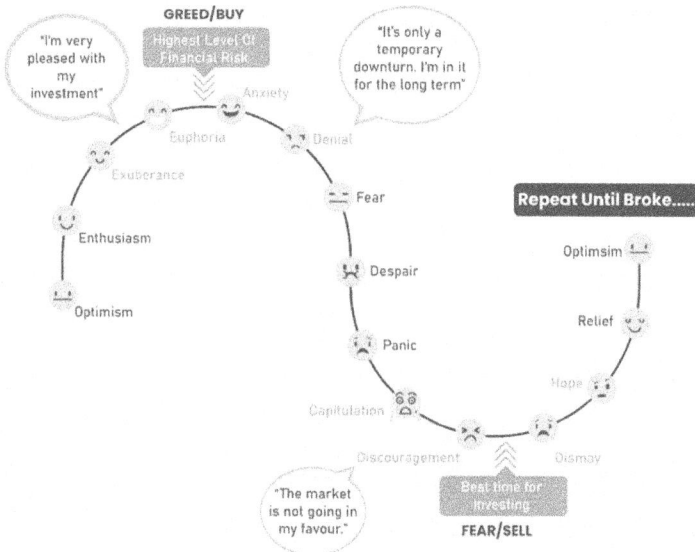

Euphoria may make you feel that it's the right time to invest more. Traders should be very cautious when relying on this emotion because, in scenarios where euphoria presents itself, almost everyone else is buying as well. This will push prices up, resulting in unrealistic over-performance in the market. People watching the cryptocurrency from the sidelines may jump in without really understanding why it is going up. There is a phrase for this FOMO or Fear Of Missing Out.

Fear occurs as a result of trading too big or entering into a trade that doesn't fit your trading plans. A trader who is consumed by fear may second guess their decisions or be overly cautious about trading actions that may incur losses. Traders that invest using a plan and invest in small amounts are less stressed because they've decided how much they're willing to risk.

When losses occur, many traders are caught up in a holding bias. They are in denial and ignore the mounting losses as the price decreased because they can't accept the loss. Traders should learn to accept such losses and move on. This book focuses on looking at patterns to alert traders of a downturn before they suffer large losses.

As the price continues to drop, nervous traders holding onto the asset may panic and overlook the reasons that convinced them to buy the investment in the first place.

Capitulation is near the bottom of the cycle and is the point where many people have given up, sold their cryptocurrency, and accepted their loss. They may be so discouraged at this point that they never invest in cryptocurrencies such as Bitcoin again.

Trading Philosophy

If there is no conviction or excitement in every trade you enter into, then this is not the right trade for you and your trading plans.

When you feel more confident about a trade, there are probably reasons for that optimism and you will make a realistic assessment of the trade.

If you only want to enter into trades that will result in big wins, then you're becoming greedy. Maybe you've been doing well and getting higher returns, but if you're not careful, this exuberance will be your downfall. Use proper trading strategies like setting stop-loss orders, profit targets, and good risk management mechanisms to avoid any large losses resulting from your overconfidence.

Sometimes a seemingly good trade will still result in losses while a bad trade may still incur gains. Always be optimistic about every trade because you might win regardless. You will need to accept this and take the time to understand why the trade didn't perform as you expected.

Learn from your mistakes and as you gain more experience you will start winning more often than losing when you trade.

Cryptocurrency Supply And Demand

Many countries use fiat currency as a form of trading. The central government and other monetary reserves control the supply of fiat currency. Thus, it's considered legal tender. On the other hand, cryptocurrency uses a decentralized network. There is no central authority or government control over it, and as a result, many entities do not accept cryptocurrency as legal tender.

Bitcoin has a fixed supply and factors such as inflation, economic growth, and monetary policies do not have any effect. Only 21 million Bitcoin will ever be created which is enforced by the computer code behind Bitcoin.

Other cryptocurrencies such as Ethereum may not have a fixed supply. Ethereum has been artificially limited to 100 million but could be changed.

Bitcoin supply and market demand influence Bitcoin prices. Other factors that influence Bitcoin prices include

- The cost of mining a Bitcoin
- The number of other available cryptocurrencies
- The exchange website for trading Bitcoin
- Regulations that govern the sale of Bitcoin

Supply and demand are the major factors determining cryptocurrency prices. Newly mined Bitcoin has a fixed rate, and the mined Bitcoin is slowly introduced to the market. This results in a situation where demand is high and supply is low, hence, driving prices up.

On the other hand, if the supply is high and the demand is low, then the price of the cryptocurrency coin will drop. The price can also be influenced by the popularity of other competing cryptocurrencies.

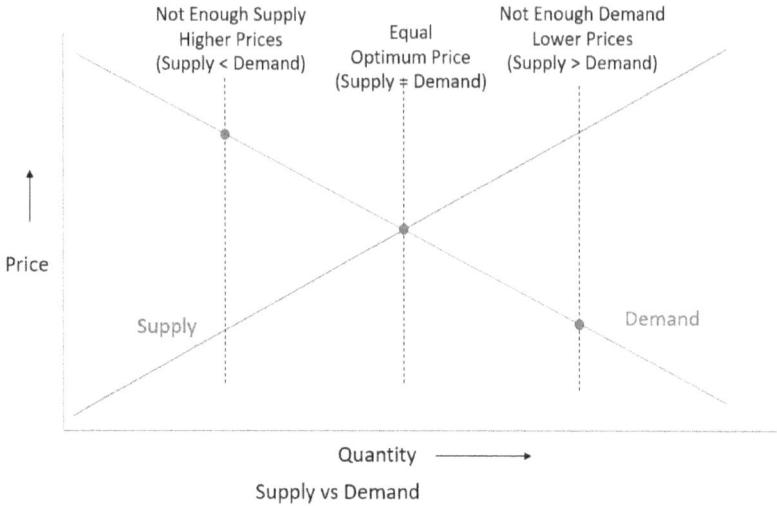

Supply vs Demand

Identifying supply and demand zones can boost your trading. A scenario with more sellers than buyers available indicates a supply zone, whereas a situation with more buyers than sellers is a demand zone.

CryptoCurrency vs. Stock Market

Many people describe the cryptocurrency market and the stock market as if they are the same, but the similarity between the two is mainly limited to the fact that prices in both systems are determined based on demand.

Most cryptocurrencies require a low entry fee even though the exchange may charge a fee for buying and selling. Investing in stocks and cryptocurrencies with low prices can result in higher yields. Trading in safer environments and monitoring price movements contribute to the success of your investment.

Although there are similarities between the two market systems, there are also some differences. Some of these differences include:

- **Fractional Purchases:** Most stocks can only be bought in whole amounts. If the stock is $55/share, you must pay $55 to buy the share of stock. In cryptocurrency, anyone can buy fractions of a Bitcoin or Ethereum. Investor Betty can purchase $100 of Bitcoin which translates to 0.01176 Bitcoin if the price of Bitcoin is $8500.

- **Market volatility:** Compared to the traditional stock market, cryptocurrency assets are highly volatile making them easily manipulated. Coin prices can change rapidly within a single day as they can either increase to 100 times the original price or decrease to 1/100th of the original value.

- **24/7 market:** Cryptocurrencies use peer to peer networks. Thus, you can trade them at any time of the day and from anywhere in the world. The prices change every minute or hour, and the markets are open 24/7. The traditional stock market, on the other hand, has set trading hours available during the business day.

- **Security:** If you buy traditional stocks, you must also buy security insurance based on your state laws. In cryptocurrency, however, once the transaction has been done, it cannot be reversed. As a result of this, when an exchange is hacked, the hackers send the crypto to themselves and the customers may not get their money or cryptocurrency back.

- **Inconsistent Prices:** Cryptocurrency prices change more often than traditional stocks since no central authority exists to control prices or set price limits. The prices are unstable, and crypto traders need to monitor the price movements and find the best exchanges before making any investment decisions. Different exchanges may have different prices for the cryptocurrency which can be exploited as described in the arbitrage section.

Cryptocurrency Exchanges

Cryptocurrency exchange platforms and websites allow traders to convert their digital currencies into other digital currencies or convert to fiat money. Traders can buy, sell, or even exchange digital currency into traditional ones like dollars or euros. Cryptocurrency exchanges have become an important part of the ownership of crypto-asset ecosystems.

The rise of cryptocurrency exchange companies does not pose a threat to the financial stability of any country. It can, however, influence consumer protection and prompt the intervention of regulatory bodies to avoid any money laundering cases.

Types of exchanges

• **Direct Trading:** In this type of exchange, individuals rely on the exchange platform to trade directly with each other. A trader can exchange his or her currency of choice with that of another trader from a different country. In direct trading, there is no fixed market price and each seller is free to set his or her exchange rate.

• **Trading Platforms:** This is a website that connects currency buyers with currency sellers. The website owners benefit from the transaction fee charged from each transaction.

• **Brokers:** These are third-party websites that anyone can visit to purchase cryptocurrency based on the broker's set price.

Factors to Consider Before Choosing a Cryptocurrency Exchange

Before you start trading, you need to research the best platforms and consider what they have to offer. Some factors to look at include:

• **Fees:** Look at the transaction fee-related information from the exchange website. Make sure you know how much they charge for deposits, withdrawals, and transactions. Different exchange programs charge different fees. Compare each program's costs, and choose one favorable to your needs. Fees are particularly important for day traders since they can easily eat into profits.

• **Site reputation:** Look for website reviews from other users, and read what they say about the website. You can also ask questions in forums such as Reddit or BitcoinTalk. Some exchanges have been scams where the owners disappeared with investor's Bitcoin.

• **Payment options:** Look at the various payment options available on the website. Do they accept PayPal, wire transfer, debit, or credit? If they have limited payment options, then it may not be the most convenient site for you to use. Credit cards require verifying your identity and attract a higher premium due to the higher risks and processing fees involved. Wire transfers may take a long time to process transactions, depending on the banks involved.

• **Exchange rate:** Each cryptocurrency exchange platform charges different rates. Shop around different exchange platforms before trading and you might be surprised to see how much you can save.

- **<u>Verification requirements:</u>** Cryptocurrency trading websites require ID verification before making any cryptocurrency deposits or withdrawals. Other sites may require anonymity, and if so, it may take a few days before the transaction is processed as the exchange platform has to be protected from money laundering and other scams.

- **<u>Geographical limitations</u>:** Some exchange platforms are restricted to certain countries. Be sure the exchange platform you want to join offers all the services to your country.

Cryptocurrency Exchange Examples

Cryptocurrency Exchange Examples

Kraken

Kraken is one of the largest Bitcoin exchange platforms. The platform allows users to buy and sell Bitcoin and trade them with either US or Canadian Dollars, Euros, the Japanese Yen, or Pounds. Kraken supports other cryptocurrencies as well.

Pros

- Low transaction fee
- Good reputation
- Excellent user support
- Worldwide support

Cons

- Not suitable for beginners
- Limited payment options

###

Coinbase

Coinbase is one of the most popular and trusted cryptocurrency exchange platforms in the world. The platform allows its users to buy, sell, and store digital currency. You can access your digital wallet account from any device, and trade Bitcoin with other digital currencies.

Pros

- Beginner-friendly platform
- Charges lower transaction fees
- Secure transactions
- Highly trusted by millions of users due to its good reputation

Cons

- Limited payment options
- Supported in only a few countries

###

ChangeNow

ChangeNow is a reliable currency exchange platform offering great exchange rates to users. You do not have to open a new account to exchange currency and can buy a wide range of coins from the platform at low cost. There are not any hidden charges either.

Pros

- Doesn't require an account
- No transaction limits
- Over 170 cryptocurrency coins are listed in the platform
- Provides 24/7 customer support

Cons

- Doesn't offer any leverage while trading coins

###

Bitbuy.ca

Bitbuy.ca is a Canadian digital exchange platform that provides secure access to Bitcoin and other digital currencies. The platform is great for long-term traders who want to buy and hold digital assets for a certain period. It is suitable for Canadian traders who want to buy or quickly convert their fiat money to cryptocurrency.

Pros

- Excellent customer services
- Quick process of transactions (both deposits and withdrawals)
- Quick customer registration and verification.
- Suitable for beginners and experienced users

Cons

- Only available in Canada

###

Shapeshift

Shapeshift is a reliable platform for those who want to quickly exchange coins without registering for an account. Traders don't have to rely on the website to hold digital currency. The website doesn't have any fiat policy, and users can easily exchange Bitcoin with other currencies supported by the platform.

Pros

- Instant exchange of the currency.
- Great interface suitable for beginners
- Fair transaction fees

Cons

- No exchange to fiat money
- Limited payment options

Binance

Binance is one of the first cryptocurrency exchange platforms to allow automated trading integration. The platform allows its users to buy, sell, and store digital currency. You can use their API to connect an automated trading platform to their exchange to buy and sell crypto automatically.

Pros

- Beginner-friendly platform
- Charges lower transaction fees
- Secure transactions
- API for automated trading

Cons

- Limited payment options
- Supported in only a few countries

Localbitcoins

Localbitcoins was the first platform to match buyers and

sellers locally. Think of it like Craigslist for Bitcoin. If you want to buy Bitcoin, you can contact a seller from a list of sellers in your area. The sellers have reviews so you can select reputable sellers.

Pros

- Fairly anonymous (KYC/AML checks for transactions > 1000 Euro)
- Can buy with cash

Cons

- Some sellers require meeting in person
- Limited payment options
- Usually higher buy prices than exchanges.

Cryptocurrency Regulation

Bitcoin and other cryptocurrencies are not regulated in the same manner as traditional stocks and bonds because they do not meet the necessary regulation criteria.

Stock exchange markets require that companies selling stock security educate investors about the health of the business they've invested in. Bitcoin developers do not have that same obligation to educate traders because it uses a decentralized network and no single entity or corporation is in control of it.

Due to its decentralized nature, it is difficult to identify Bitcoin promoters and force them to make any disclosures. Using a disclosure regime as required by federal security laws does not add any value to Bitcoin.

Companies that deal with cryptocurrency exchanges comply with tax and banking regulations, which are aimed at protecting consumers. Thus, the security regulations on cryptocurrency do not give any benefits to the investors.

Manipulation

Bitcoin Whales

In the cryptocurrency world, a whale can be an individual, group, or institution that holds a large number of the cryptocurrency coins. Whales act as market players and represent the major Bitcoin influencers in the market. These players manipulate the market since they come in and buy a high number of available Bitcoins, reducing the overall supply. As a result, they drive Bitcoin prices up.

When the price increases up to their target level, whales sell the assets and get higher returns. They may do so for a while, and their actions force the asset price to fall back to its acceptable level.

Since Bitcoin is very expensive, not everyone can become a Bitcoin whale. Bitcoin miners can become Bitcoin whales when they have created a bunch of Bitcoin and go through the high maintenance demands of Bitcoin mining. Many early adopters who bought or mined Bitcoin when it was less than $1 are also Bitcoin whales.

Bitcoin whales drive prices up and down, and investors should observe these patterns to maximize their returns. Knowing when whales are entering the market or when the price momentum is slowing down will help you make money as an investor.

How Much Do Whales Own?

The biggest whale is Bitcoin inventor, Satoshi Nakamoto, who owns over a million Bitcoins. Analysts believe these Bitcoins are lost forever since they have not circulated since he mined them.

Research conducted by Diar.co in 2017 estimates that 55% of the circulating Bitcoin is controlled by around 1600 investors.

There are four categories that Bitcoin whales fall into. According to Chainalysis.com, they include:

Trader Whales: These institutions hold 332,000 BTC with an estimated value of $2.1 billion. The BTC are spread across nine wallets, and they have been actively trading Bitcoin since 2017.

Trader whales buy Bitcoin when prices fall, mostly through their induction. They manipulate the market conditions to purchase large numbers of Bitcoin at lower costs.

Bitcoin Miners and Investors: This group of whales owns a collection of Bitcoin held in 15 e-wallets. The whales hold about 332,000 BTC, the same number as the trader whales.

Lost whales: These whales hold 212,000 BTC valued at $1.3 billion. The BTC are spread across five e-wallets. These types of whales are so-called "lost" because they are known to be early Bitcoin owners who have either since died or lost the keys to their e-wallets.

Criminal whales: This group holds 12,000 BTC spread across three wallets. The BTC are estimated to value $790 million, and their transaction activity is connected to dark spheres like money laundering and other illegal activities.

Cryptocurrency Pump And Dump

Trader whales don't appear to have a significant impact on

cryptocurrency liquidity. These active communities of Bitcoin traders could influence the market price of Bitcoin. If they decide to dump a large amount of BTC in the market when the price of cryptocurrency is high, then there will be a drop in the value of Bitcoin and this can directly affect the Bitcoin exchange rate.

All Bitcoin purchases made in that period may result in a loss to the investor.

The biggest whales in the market tend to analyze the market trends and study the behavior of other Bitcoin owners before making their next actions. Therefore, the Bitcoin whale "club" of active Bitcoin owners tends to spread out the huge "dumping" of Bitcoins into several thousand smaller transactions that don't affect the price as much as large transactions.

Criminals are more likely to "dump" a large number of coins on the market since their cost was low which means any price is fair and they want to get out before government coin tracking improves.

Both pump and dump buying patterns lead to rising and falling prices every time a player takes an action. As such, "pumping and dumping" leads to the introduction of cheap coins in the market.

The market players will create hype around a crypto-coin so that more investors will be interested in buying the coins. When investors start to buy in large numbers, the prices of the crypto-coin go up, fueling the pumping process. Bitcoin is large enough that this doesn't appear to be a common issue.

Traders need to be aware of this possibility and should be

watching to recognize the pump and dump characteristics.

Chapter Summary

In this chapter, you learned about the cryptocurrency market and why Bitcoin is the most traded cryptocurrency. Bitcoin and other cryptocurrency coins are traded on TradingView, which provides real-time data on the cryptocurrency market.

The cryptocurrency TradingView platform helps investors gather the real-time information they need to successfully trade crypto assets. Tools such as TradingView help them determine when to enter the market and when to exit. Also, these tools show them how to take advantage of inherent market volatility to increase cryptocurrency returns.

Traders will have an upper hand when choosing the right cryptocurrency exchange platform to convert their fiat currency to cryptocurrency and invest in crypto assets. There are different exchange platforms in the market, and this guide listed a few of the most popular ones. You have to look at the various factors of each exchange platform and weigh its advantages and disadvantages before choosing the one suitable for your trading needs.

> **TO GET HIGHER PROFITS FROM THE SALE OF THE ASSETS, TRADERS SHOULD CONSTANTLY MONITOR THE DEMAND AND SUPPLY OF CRYPTOCURRENCIES SUCH AS BITCOIN. THEY SHOULD ALSO TAKE ADVANTAGE OF TIMES WHERE BITCOIN WHALES ENTER INTO THE MARKET. INVESTORS SHOULD LEARN HOW TO AVOID PUMP AND DUMP SITUATIONS.**

CHAPTER 3
Strategies for Making Money in Cryptocurrency

Intro

A trading strategy involves buying and selling cryptocurrency assets using predefined rules.

A good trading strategy should have a well-thought-out plan with specific trading objectives, a trading time-frame, and a risk tolerance plan.

The plan involves developing methods aimed at buying and selling crypto assets. It should also have a strategy that meets your investment goals. Trading strategies help identify the entry and exit points in the crypto market.

Cryptocurrency Investment Strategies

Buy & Hold

Buy and hold (sometimes referred to as HODL) is the basic trading strategy where you buy the crypto asset, hold it, and later sell it. To hold the asset requires a lot of confidence. You have to be optimistic about the rising prices to hold the asset and sell at a higher price later. The investor holds the asset as long as the prices are rising. The bull market fuels the buy and hold strategy.

HODL means "Hold On For Dear Life" and has been used in

the Bitcoin crypto-sphere to indicate the buy and hold strategy for cryptocurrency investments. Holding the coin for a certain period can result in long-term benefits to the crypto traders.

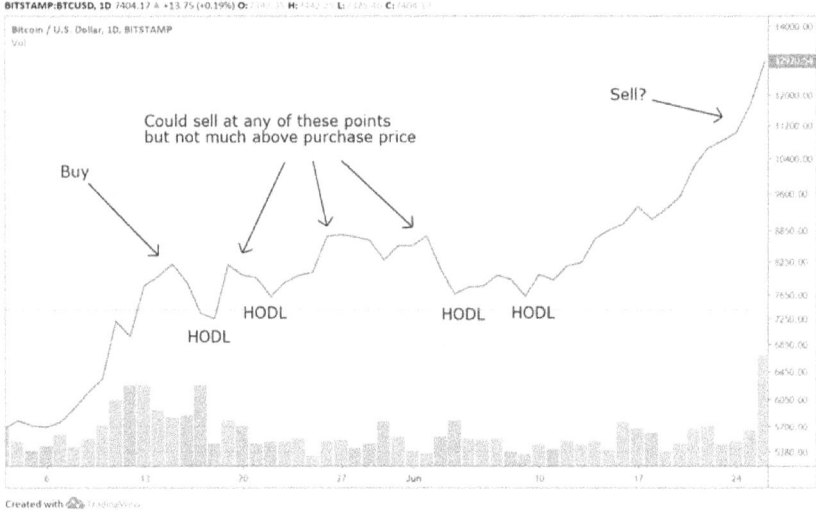

Many HODL investors have been able to achieve their long-term business goals. Investing in multiple cryptocurrencies such as Ethereum, EOS, Ripple, etc is one way to diversify the investment risks.

As cryptocurrencies increase in value, the gains are not as large as they are for lower-priced cryptocurrencies. Right now, an investor can buy almost 50 Ethereum for the same price as 1 Bitcoin. This spread varies, at the Bitcoin/Ethereum price peak, it was about 20:1. Diversifying the cryptocurrency portfolio can result in better returns and also re-balance the portfolio.

Most Buy and Hold investors do not set a stop-loss. A stop-loss would set a sell order if the price dropped an amount that is uncomfortable for the investor. However, setting a stop-loss removes the emotion from the trade. It locks in the loss but prevents an even larger loss by a stubborn investor. Setting stops to limit the downside is recommended by most successful investors.

Advantages of the Buy and Hold Strategy in a Bull Market

1. Reduces market noise by 95%

The long-term bull trend line helps bolster the buy and hold trading strategy since it reduces the market noise brought up by a lower trading term. Short-term trading patterns are usually unpredictable, which can affect trades. A weekly chart line on price actions is non-volatile for a certain period.

2.Reduced transaction costs

• Long-term traders using the buy and hold method do not over-trade. This technique significantly reduces transaction costs. On the other hand, a short-term trader engaged in weekly or daily trades has to account for each trade's accumulated transaction cost as well.

• Trading on several short-term trades will be very expensive compared to executing a few long-term trades.

3.Reduces psychological strain

• Executing several short-term or medium-term trades can be very stressful, especially if the trader is less experienced. The buy and hold method is less stressful than short-term trades. While it can still be stressful, the buy and hold method is much better than the short trading strategy.

4. Perfect market timing is not important

• The buy and hold strategy is attractive to many traders

because market timing is not important. Traders can enter into the market without being on guard for a major pullback against an incoming bull market trend. Long-term investors know that they can miss potential opportunities if they rely on perfect market timing.

5. Time efficiency

• The buy and hold trading method is ideal for investors aiming for higher gains with minimal time expenditure. Long-term investors don't have to constantly monitor price changes daily or use technical analysis charts to watch price movements. Still, they should always keep track of fundamental news in the cryptocurrency market and check their position every so often to benefit from their crypto-asset investment.

6. Lower taxes

• Holding crypto assets for a long period results in great capital gains. Investments held at least a year before selling are eligible for lower taxes. The assets attract long-term tax rates instead of higher short-term rates.

7. Dollar-Cost Averaging

• A Buy and Hold investor will typically invest on a regular schedule like each week or each month. Many investors buy $100 of Bitcoin every month. As the price goes up and down, the result is averaged. If the long term trend is a bull market, the investor will see an increase in their assets.

Tips For Successful HODL Cryptocurrency Trading

• Traders should use a large time frame like weekly and monthly charts to perform technical analysis.

- Watch out for the factors that influence long-term goals of Bitcoin trading.

- Taking advantage of the pullback strategy will enable you to obtain a better entry price point.

- Avoid holding leveraged crypto coins for a long time since it can be costly. If used, minimize the leverage.

- When using stop-loss orders, you should not place it too close to the entry.

- Dollar-cost average to even out the high and low price fluctuations.

Investors using HODL should guard their investments against potential market crashes and understand how to take advantage of the bull market to utilize profits and cut losses. These investors can benefit from understanding the techniques in this book.

Bitcoin Mining Strategy

The process of creating new coins is called mining. Mining Bitcoin (or other crypto coins) is another way to obtain coins. Unfortunately, Bitcoin mining has progressed to the point where custom hardware "rigs" are needed.

However, you can mine less popular coins using second-hand rigs and exchange the coins for Bitcoin on the exchange website. You can also hold the coins for a while and sell when the price increases.

Miners have the expense of buying an operating the rigs. In some cases, this can be a significant cost in electricity and cooling costs since the rigs create heat while running.

Arbitraging Strategy

In an arbitrage strategy, you buy the coins at a lower price and sell them at a higher price in a different location. As an example, the price of Bitcoin is $8500 on Coinbase and $8600 on Binance. Buying 1 Bitcoin on Coinbase and then selling 1 Bitcoin on Binance could return a profit of $100 minus the Binance and Coinbase fees.

This is less viable now because the technique is now widely known. Some companies and people are constantly scanning for price discrepancies and are more likely to act quickly than you.

However, this may be a good technique with less well-known coins.

Passive Income from Dividend Payouts Strategy

I hesitated before including this strategy because there have been many scams around "renting" your coins. Do your homework on the companies that advertise dividends because the vast majority of these have been scams that take your cryptocurrency and leave you with nothing.

I'm including it here because it is a viable strategy if you use a reputable company.

In some cases, lending cryptocurrency coins can earn dividends between 5% and 10% per year. These dividends are usually limited to a few coins like Bitcoin, NEO, and VeChain. If the coin price goes up for a certain period, you gain more profits.

Recently, coins that use Proof-of-Stake instead of Proof-of-Work can earn dividends while held in cryptocurrency exchanges such as Coinbase, Bittrex, or Kraken.

Trading Strategy

Trading is the primary theme of this book so this chapter will focus more on trading than the other strategies.

Long Trade

A long trade is a term used when purchasing cryptocurrency assets at a cheaper price with the expectation of selling them at a high price in the future to gain profit.

Day traders can also use a long trade strategy when they buy the asset with the expectation that the price will rise during the day and then sell. "Buy" and "long" are common terms in the trading sector. If an investor says, "Going long," it means he or she has an interest in buying a particular asset and holding onto it with the expectation that it will increase in value.

Long trades have unlimited profit gains since the price of the coin can go up indefinitely.

Short Trade

In a short trade, the coin is sold because the trader expects the price to decrease. If the coin isn't owned, traders can borrow the coin for a fee. This is called a "naked" short and is only recommended for experienced traders since the price could go up.

In a "naked" short trade, the trader sells the borrowed coin to repurchase it later at a lower price and return the coin to the person it was borrowed from. If the selling price is higher than what they re-purchase it at, they keep the profit.

Short sales have high financial risks. Be very careful when using this strategy because sometimes key market players can drive the price up, forcing short position speculators to buy back the asset before the price goes too high. This is referred to as a "short squeeze" and ironically, this can cause the price to zoom even higher since there are more buyers.

Typical Trading Strategies

It is hard to determine when prices are at a peak or valley, but you can use the following strategies to take advantage of the bull and bear markets.

Choosing A Trading Timeframe

Trading charts are drawn on different time-frames or even sometimes with other data like price range or the number of trades made. Charts can show minute, hourly, daily, or weekly data. Based on your needs and the type of cryptocurrency used, you can choose either a long time-frame or a short time-frame. The trading time-frame chosen depends on your personality.

If you want to make many trades within a single day, you can choose a short time frame. If you only do one or two trades per week, then you can choose a longer time frame.

Long Term Traders

Long-term traders rely on either daily or weekly charts to make trading decisions. Weekly trading charts identify the long-term trends and help set the trading plan. In this form of trading, you don't have to monitor price changes throughout the day.

The daily charts are useful for determining the entry and exit points, while a monthly chart can be used to determine the primary market trend. Traders and investors will also have enough time to evaluate each trade before taking action.

Day Traders

A daily trader can rely on 5, 15, or 60-minute charts to identify the primary market trend. The five-minute charts indicate a short-term trend. These charts show the specific points where traders should take action and enter or exit the trend market.

Traders using the day trading strategy always have to be tuned in. Not doing so can negatively impact your profitability. For this reason, brokers and other third-party firms offer user-friendly apps accessible via mobile devices.

Day trading is a short-term trading technique where you can hold the asset for a few hours and sell it with the hopes of getting positive returns. Chart analysis allows traders to monitor the price movement of the cryptocurrency and predict future direction based on its historical data.

Day Trading

Cryptocurrency day trading involves buying and selling crypto assets at a profit. The practice has become popular in recent years due to high volatility and trading volumes.

Daily crypto trading is characterized by high risk. Before you enter into any trade, you have to know where to take profits. You also need to know the price to stop the trade to avoid major losses. Smart investors control the size of their position in the market. They also do not risk a significant portion of their investment portfolio or use too much leverage in a single trade.

To succeed in day trading, you have to be tuned in constantly.

Receiving any big news or announcements just a few minutes later than everyone else can result in huge profits or losses.

Types of Day Traders

Day traders use different approaches to achieve their trading goals. They can either be speculators or technical analysts.

Speculators

The speculators find the outside factors that influence the price of the cryptocurrency. They look for indicators such as news events to predict the gain or loss of cryptocurrency asset values.

There are several user-friendly mobile apps designed to ensure you're constantly updated about what's happening in the cryptocurrency world. As a speculator, you have to spend a considerable amount of time on your preferred cryptocurrency platform daily and cryptocurrency news sites, so choose an app that meets your investment needs and trading style.

Technical Analysts

Technical analysis is more concerned about the market itself than any external influences affecting asset pricing. Technical analyst traders use financial charts and patterns to predict price movement. Learning how to use technical analysis tools will give you a better idea of the direction of coin prices. Knowing how to read chart lines and patterns is very important for any day trader.

A day trading strategy is not a get-rich-quick scheme. It has many risks, and you are likely to lose a lot of money before fully understanding how the strategy works. Even experienced traders prefer making small profits over a large number of trades with this method.

When buying cryptocurrencies, you need to compare the different types of brokers and what they offer. Select brokers who offer cryptocurrency trades with lower fees for frequent trading because day trades have many trades in a day and the fees can erode profitable trades.

Getting Started in Day Trading

After deciding to day trading, you need to choose a home exchange for your currency. When choosing a home exchange, remember that different exchanges provide different fee structures, have various minimum trade restrictions, and offer different coin pairings.

The fee structure influences the volume of trade. If your trading style involves trading in large volumes, you may only get small profits from the trade, since part of the profit will pay for the trading fees.

Once you have registered your account for daily trading, develop a trading strategy. Research the coin you want to invest in, as well as any relevant news or technical analysis about it and its market.

Set ground rules for day trading. For example, set a rule that restricts you from risking more than 1% of your predetermined investment on a single trade. Successful day trading requires discipline; without it, you will incur huge losses.

Set stop-loss limits. A stop-loss limit is an important factor when setting up a trading strategy, and it acts as your exit strategy. Setting the limit to a particular level will allow your exchange program to automatically exit the trade after attaining that level. If you buy 0.01 Bitcoin for $100, you can set the stop loss to $80. This will ensure you don't lose more than 20% of your investment by automatically selling the coins to preserve 80% of your investment in case the coin price falls. One thing to note is that during a panic, there will be a lot of people trying to sell and the stop loss may sell at a lower price than you selected. Luckily panics are rare events but they need to be considered a part of day trading.

You can also limit the sell orders. This will automatically close a trade once the coin reaches a price level you select. If the coin price is on an upward trend and you bought 0.01 Bitcoin for $100, you can set a sell limit order to $130 to ensure you lock in the gains. Setting the limit order will ensure the coin is sold automatically when the price level reaches $130 which would be a 30% profit. It is always good to have an exit value in mind when you make a trade.

Don't second guess yourself if the price continues higher, a profit is always a win.

Trading volatility

Volatility describes the change in prices of an asset - either moving up or down very quickly. The price direction can result in higher gains or losses to traders. The prices are sensitive to regulatory changes and highly dependent on daily crypto news and announcements.

Bitcoin prices can rise and fall anywhere from 5% to 50% within a single day, whereas the prices of traditional markets such as the New York Stock Exchange (NYSE) typically do not change as much in the same time-frame. Trading volatility is a distinguishing factor between day trading cryptocurrency and day trading other general assets.

Traditional day traders typically sell their positions before the stock market closes since news after the close can have a large impact. Although cryptocurrency exchanges are open 24 hours a day, 7 days a week, limiting the holding window is a good habit for crypto traders as well.

Traders can take advantage of the volatile market and make good returns on their investments, but doing so involves a keen willingness to make risky moves and accept high losses.

Day Trading Taxes

The taxes paid on Bitcoin assets depend on the length of time you held the asset. Different countries have different tax laws that govern different tax views on cryptocurrency assets. Therefore, perform due diligence and follow the tax laws for your country.

In the United States, if you hold a crypto asset for less than a year, the transaction will be taxed at your normal income tax rate. When you buy crypto assets with fiat currency, you're not liable to pay taxes on the purchase transaction (until it is sold).

When you sell cryptocurrency assets, you have to pay income tax for every sell transaction. By default, you are taxed using the First In First Out (FIFO) method. In the FIFO method, your first sale will be matched to the price of the first purchase and you will pay tax on the amount of gain. There is also a Last In First Out (LIFO) method that may affect taxes so consult a tax professional.

If you hold a Bitcoin asset for more than a year, it will be classified as a capital gain under US tax laws and the asset will be taxed at a lower rate (currently 15%). Capital gain taxes are typically lower than most people's regular income taxes. Most day traders won't be able to use this lower tax rate because they buy and sell so frequently.

Day Trading Considerations

1.Volatility

• Day trading cryptocurrency prices move up and down quickly and can either lead to higher profits or loss, unlike stock asset prices. The price of a coin can rise and fall 10% to 50% or even more in a single day.

2.Accept losses

• Day trading Bitcoin or any other cryptocurrency may not work as expected. Sometimes you have losses while others make profits. You need to accept losses once they occur; this is part of trading. You will not make the correct prediction every time, and even the most experienced traders make wrong predictions.

• If you have losses, don't try to recover it by taking even higher risks. This will lead to failure. You should always accept losses and then evaluate what went wrong and course-correct for the next transaction.

3.Practice first

• Before investing in real money, you need to practice first. Although not all exchange platforms offer you a demo account, the CryptoHopper and Coins2Learn platforms provide a trading simulator to practice trading. The platforms give tips to new traders on how to be successful in trading. Keep in mind that they make money with the up-sell so you will get a lot of emails, etc.

• You can paper trade using a notebook to track when you buy and sell and at what prices. Once you are satisfied that you understand the market, go ahead and invest with real money.

• When beginning to trade, it's recommended to start with small amounts. That is, an amount you can afford to lose since paper trading/simulation doesn't prepare you for real-world losses.

• As you continue trading, you will hone your skills along with a better understanding of the highs and lows of the trending market.

4.Set targets

• After learning how the market works and its ups and downs, you can set targets for yourself. You need a plan for your expectations at the end of the day. Targets should be focused - such as how much of a loss you can absorb, how much of a gain before selling, how long to stay in a trade, and a safe stop-loss value.

• Day trading has short-term gains which can be as low as 1% per trade. Several gains each day can increase your bank amount and help you build a steady income.

5.Use Stop-losses

• Stop-losses are an essential factor in day trading cryptocurrency. A stop-loss is a value set so that if you were expecting the price to increase but the coin price drops to that stop-loss point, you automatically exit the trade. It is used to prevent more losses.

• If you bought Bitcoin for $6000, you can set a stop-loss at 10%. Then, if the price of Bitcoin drops to $5400, the system automatically sells the investment on your behalf. If you're not online when the prices drop, the stop-loss will save you from incurring further losses automatically.

• You can also use limit sell orders, which allow the system to automatically sell your Bitcoin or close a trade after Bitcoin hits the set higher price. In this case, if you set a limit sell order to 10%, the coin will automatically be sold when the price hit $6600.

6.Choose appropriate trading bots

• Based on your trading needs, choose a trading bot that helps you become more successful. Compare different trading bots in terms of their reputation, fees, cost, features, and other essential factors based on your desired use.

• **Note:** When day trading, you have to be calm throughout despite the rushed time-frames. You should keep the following in mind:

• You shouldn't be greedy

• Don't trade an amount you're not ready to lose

• Don't move from one strategy to another. You should always evaluate your success and failure before making any changes otherwise you are not learning from your successes and losses.

Bull & Bear Market

A bull market occurs when crypto asset prices are expected to rise during a particular trading period. In the stock market, the prices of securities rise and fall continuously over a particular trading term. The bull market indicates that the prices of various securities are rising for an extended period, usually over months or years.

The upward trend results in higher gains in the crypto market. In a bull market, investors buy more coins to increase their profits.

Although it is difficult to predict changes in market trends, investors relying on bull markets are confident and optimistic about higher returns for an extended period. A bull market is characterized by higher highs and lower lows - a concept that is explained in more detail later in this book.

In the stock market, a bull market is an indicator of expansion in the economy. Typically economic conditions affect the prices of security assets traded.

Cryptocurrency is seen as a safe haven and many times, bad economic data will result in Bitcoin and other crypto-currencies increasing in price. This is another reason that cryptocurrency is good to have in your portfolio for diversity.

Investors can take advantage of a bull market by buying crypto assets when prices start to rise and selling them when the price is at its peak.

A bear market is characterized by a period of downward price movement. The price falling results in a downward trend.

In a cryptocurrency bear market, traders are more likely to sell their assets than purchase additional ones. During this trading term, you can expect to see both lower highs and lower lows in the trend lines.

Tips for Cryptocurrency Trading

Have a purpose for each trade

Before placing any trade, you need to have a reason as to why you want to trade crypto assets. In the cryptocurrency market, there is always a winner and a loser. It is a zero-sum game; for every win, there is a corresponding loss.

Whether you're a day trader or long-term trader, you must be patient. Don't rush a trade and cause losses. sometimes it's better to make a small gain than rush into losses with a single trade.

Set profit targets and stop-loss orders

You should always know when to enter and exit the market and how much profit you want to make. If you plan to get out of the market when you make a certain profit or if the price hits a set target, stick to that plan. Don't be greedy.

Place stop-loss orders to help you cut down on losses. When trading, put emotions aside and set a stop-loss point so that when the price drops to the stop-loss points, the asset is sold automatically.

Manage Risks

You need to learn how to manage risk in the business. It's better to accumulate a low amount of profit from small, regular trades than to risk everything by investing big. If the market is less liquid, invest small amounts and set both stop-loss and profit targets further from the buying price.

Welcome FOMO

FOMO (fear of missing out) is trading psychology experienced by traders and one of the reasons why the majority of traders fail. There are times when almost everyone wants to trade, and you feel like jumping into the market by buying the coins. Bitcoin whales are watching every move that small traders are making. This will lead to an oversupply of coins in the market, and the price will drop as demand vanishes.

If you can harness your emotions, you can exploit the FOMO and sell when you see that people are in FOMO mode.

Don't Buy Because The Price Is Low

Buying coins because the price is low is one common mistake made by beginning traders. You need to look for other factors before buying the coin. You shouldn't base the decision to buy the coin on its affordability. You should look at the market cap of the coin. The higher the cap, the more suitable to invest in it.

Volatile Market Condition Created Through Underlying Assets

The Bitcoin price is quite volatile, and it affects the prices of other currencies. If the price of Bitcoin rises, the price of altcoins and other coins may drop since the available money is flowing into Bitcoin.

The variability of Bitcoin prices confuses traders, making it difficult to understand the market. In this case, you can set profit targets and rely on them to sell or just hold your coins while you wait for a clear market.

Be Vigilant Of ICOs

Some startups encourage the public to invest in their ICO (Initial Coin Offering) with a promise to get promoted coins at lower prices to sell at a profit. ICO's higher returns attract a large number of investors. Recently a large number of firms using ICO strategies are scams. Therefore, be careful when investing in an ICO.

Scrutinize all information provided to attract investors. Do a background check on the people behind that firm, and analyze them to see whether they can deliver as promised. Don't just buy because of the returns they're promising.

Diversify your investment

Although cryptocurrency investments can offer large returns, they're very unpredictable. A slight change in the market conditions can make them fall within a day. You can also lose everything you hold in just seconds, especially if the exchange platform is hacked. Diversification will allow you to cope with this uncertainty.

Chapter Summary

In this chapter, you learned the various cryptocurrency investment strategies you can use to make money. It also explained how you can use long trades to buy and sell Bitcoin or use shorter methods to trade.

Traders should learn how to choose the right time-frame for trading. Long-term traders rely on daily, weekly, and monthly charts to trade. The daily charts are used in setting the entry and exit points.

Short-term traders use daily chart units to monitor price trends. The trends can be set within a time interval of 5 minutes, 30 minutes, or 60 minutes. Traders using a short trade strategy can place several trades within a single day.

Traders using a day trading strategy should condition their minds to accept losses and practice before investing real money. They should set and consider other factors like profit targets and stop-loss points before they begin any trade. Having the right mindset when making trading decisions will help you trade effectively.

Are you enjoying this book - Cryptocurrency Trading: Beginners Guide to Buying and Selling Bitcoin and other Cryptocurrencies?

First of all, thank you for purchasing this book **Cryptocurrency Trading**. *I know you could have picked any number of books to read, but you picked this book and for that I am extremely grateful.*

I hope that you are feeling a little more familiar with the methods to acquire cryptocurrencies.

If you are enjoying this book, it would be really nice if you could share this book with your friends and family by posting to Facebook and Twitter.

If you are finding some benefit in reading this, I'd like to hear from you and hope that you could take some time to post a review on Amazon. Your feedback and support will help this author to greatly improve his writing craft for future projects and make this book even better.

You can follow this link to [https://www.Amazon.com/gp/customer-reviews/write-a-review.html?asin=B084DZS6TG] now.

I want you, the reader, to know that your review is very important and so, if you'd like to **leave a review**, *all you have to do is click here and away you go.*

All right, let's continue digging into the important parts of cryptocurrency trading!

CHAPTER 4
Cryptocurrency Technical Analysis

Intro

Traders in the crypto market rely on a wide range of tools to assess the strengths and weaknesses of a crypto asset. One of the most commonly used tools is technical analysis. Technical analysis of charts helps traders understand the market sentiments, price trends, and data analysis to predict future trends on Bitcoin assets. With the information provided through technical analysis, crypto traders can make the right decision on when to invest in Bitcoin.

Technical analysis (sometimes abbreviated as TA) forecasts future cryptocurrency prices and market trends based on historical data. It anticipates whether the price trends will be up (bulls) or down (bears). This is done through the use of technical indicators, which calculate the historic and current market price of an asset and analyze price trends.

Analyzing historical price charts and collected volume data determines whether the coin is undervalued or overvalued.

Technical analysis is based on the following assumptions:

1.   The price movement follows certain trends. Bitcoin prices do not change randomly but tend to follow particular trends that last for either short or long periods. It uses past performance to predict future prices.

2. Bitcoin prices are determined by multiple variables. The price movement of the coin is due to past and future demand of the coin, current market prices, and regulations governing the cryptocurrency market.

3. History tends to repeat itself. What happened in the past is used to predict what will happen in the future. Past changes can easily predict future market changes. Traders tend to behave the same way when presented with a similar market condition.

Types of Technical Analysis

There are three components used in technical analysis:

• Chart lines: Chart lines are used to indicate the points where price changes. Using historical price data, current prices, and volume data, analysts can draw charting lines to show the exact points where the prices tend to change.

• Patterns: Chart patterns predict price movement. They show the price direction and extrapolate to show where prices are headed to.

• Indicator oscillators: This analysis tool uses statistical methods to determine the buy and sell signals.

Analysts and crypto investors rely on the charts to get visual data on price trends and market momentum.

Technical Indicators

Technical indicators are investment analysis tools used to calculate and interpret market trends. Traders rely on these tools to determine the right time to invest in cryptocurrencies (crypto). Investors can receive alerts on any new investment opportunities and price changes.

Traders can know the price movement of crypto assets whether they move up, down, or sideways. The price movement is calculated using historical price data, current prices, and trading volume data.

Technical indicators are very important in analyzing cryptocurrency investments. They help investors to:

• Predict price movement and future price direction.
• Confirm market trends in the price movement of cryptocurrency assets such as Bitcoin.
• Alert investors to whether prices are going up, down, or sideways to make arrangements necessary for trade.

Cryptocurrency investors rely on these indicators to determine the short-term price movement. They also evaluate the asset's long-term price changes to determine when to enter or exit the market.

Some of the common technical indicators used include calculating Moving Averages (MA) and the Relative Strength Index (RSI). For example, you can plot a chart to show the Bitcoin price direction for 12 and 26 days, respectively.

There are several indicators to observe when analyzing a particular cryptocurrency asset. To choose the right indicator, you need to first understand how each indicator works and how each indicator will affect your investment strategy.

Because of the volatile nature of crypto assets, monitoring the price direction or Bitcoin price chart will help the investor evaluate both high and low trading patterns. If the chart assumes an upward trend, that will indicate higher trend lines whereas a downward trend indicates a series of low trend lines.

Sometimes the cryptocurrency will move sideways. In such a case, it does not move in any particular vertical direction at all. Investors should be very careful when using only one indicator such as trend lines to predict future prices since the trends can move in any form. It is much better to use 2 or more indicators as confirmation of a move up or down.

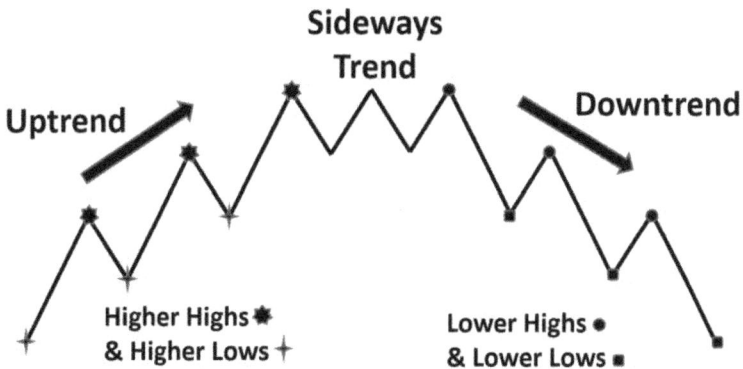

A technical analysis chart drawn based on historical prices and trading volume data represents the past decisions made by investors on the buying and selling of crypto assets. As investors, we use past data to predict future investments.

For example, a typical investor who bought Bitcoin

cryptocurrency assets will monitor the price of Bitcoin assets. If the price falls in comparison to the initial buying price, the investor may wait until the price reaches the break-even point to sell the crypto asset. As savvy investors, we recognize this as Support/Resistance explained later in this book and can use this to our advantage.

Price movement is influenced by both internal and external constraints. Multiple forces including human emotions like fear, panic, greed, anxiety, hope, and hysteria affect the prices of cryptocurrency. These emotions lead to dramatic shifts in the prices of the crypto asset. Therefore, price movement is not only based on facts but also expectations.

Trend Analysis

Trend analysis uses technical analysis tools to determine price movements and help traders know when to buy, sell, or hold a cryptocurrency asset.

This technique analyzes past cryptocurrency prices to predict future price movements. It determines an upward trend when asset prices continue to rise and detects a downward trend when prices keep decreasing over several consecutive days.

Trend lines, moving averages, and polarity analysis are the major tools used to determine price trends. In this chapter, we will focus on the use of trend lines.

Using trend lines is one of the most popular techniques used in technical analysis, and they are used to show the consistent movement of prices either up, down, or sideways. Price movement trends vary based on the time-frame and whether the investor is observing a daily, weekly, monthly or quarterly basis.

Drawing Trend Lines

Trend lines indicate the general direction of the price. Straight lines are drawn above and below the price line. Trend lines also show support and resistance areas that can determine when to enter or exit a trade. Trend lines can show increased supply or demand.

Downward trend lines are drawn above the price of the plotted chart, while upward trend lines are drawn below the price. The upward trend line is used to estimate support while the downward trendline is used to estimate resistance.

Rules of Thumb for Trend Lines

1.There must be at least two highs or lows to have a valid trend line (3 points is preferred)

• The trend line is further validated if it intersects the price line a 3rd time. Bitcoin is so volatile that it may be hard to find the 3rd point validation.

2.Larger time frames result in better trend lines.

• Start with weekly or daily charts and then check the smaller time frames to confirm.

3.Sometimes trend lines cut through the low or high portion of a candle.

- Try not to cut through the body of the candle.
- If the trend line doesn't fit without being forced, it probably isn't a valid trend.

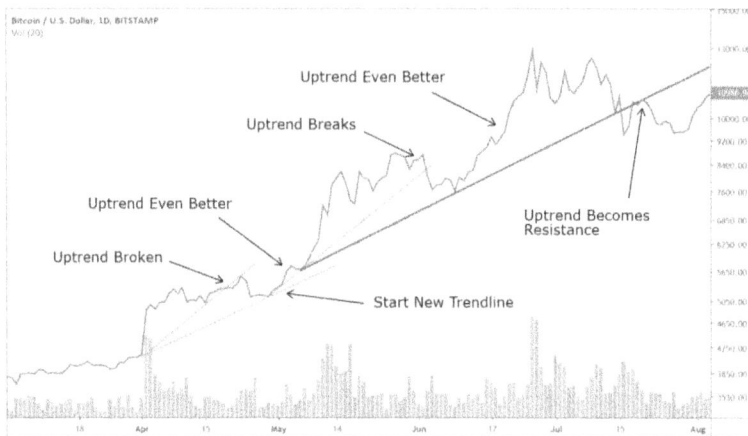

In the above chart, the prices touched the trend line at least 2 times in the given time-frame. The line represents the area of support, and it indicates when traders should be looking for buying opportunities. Sometimes the upward trendline can become a resistance line as shown on the right side.

We will discuss support and resistance in more detail below.

The downtrend touched the trend line 3 times in the given time-frame. The trend line in the graph represents resistance and indicates where the buyers are expected to slow down their buying. Traders use this to sell their crypto assets near the top.

How to Draw Trend Lines

Open the TradingView website, and then choose BTC/USD charts. This displays the real-time trending price for Bitcoin in US Dollars.

You can customize the chart and draw trend lines on it. To do so, click on the **Full-featured chart** icon to open advanced chart tools to customize your chart.

You can change the chart trend to be daily, weekly, or monthly, and then draw trend lines from the available tools. Select the Trend Line Tool on the left side of the chart.

Trading Channels

A channel consists of a pair of straight lines, with one line drawn at the top of the uptrend trend line and the other line drawn in parallel but at the bottom linking the troughs of a price series chart.

Channels are used in visualizing data to determine when to buy and sell crypto assets. The top and bottom lines are drawn to show both the support and resistance levels in the trade chart.

Trading channels show where prices will likely reverse direction. If an asset trades between the boundaries of two trend lines for a certain period, then it is trading within the channel.

If the trading price is on an uptrend, then it is an ascending channel. If the price moves downward between the trend lines, it is referred to as a descending channel. When the price moves in a range, then a horizontal channel is created.

The channel can be drawn by either using the trend lines to draw two lines or using channel tools available in the software.

Let's walk through what happened above.

When Bitcoin was at $274 (the bottom left corner of the channel), many people bought it. As a result, the price increased to $400. Investors who bought at $274 want to sell their Bitcoin at the increased price and take their profits. This leads to increased supply and less demand, which drops the Bitcoin price to $320.

At that point, investors may start buying Bitcoin expecting that the price will increase back to $400. The rise was not as rapid this time but it eventually hits $452 before the sellers take control and push the price back down to $360.

The buyers and sellers trade back and forth without much rise or fall until late May 2016 when Bitcoin becomes more attractive and rises quite fast from $450 to $750 in mid-June.

Using Channels to Make Trading Decisions

Traders rely on the channel for trading with the assumption that the price will typically remain enclosed within the channel.

If confirmed by other signals, a trader sells their Bitcoin when the price touches the upper boundary of the trend line or buys Bitcoin when the price touches the lower boundary.

Note how selling wasn't a good decision when the price touched the upper right channel because Bitcoin continued to rise. This is another example of where a good trader would realize the mistake and buy back in.

Sometimes, you may have a false breakout, which occurs when the price breaks outside the channel. In such a case, some investors may immediately buy in thinking the crypto is rocketing upwards. It is best to wait until it closes outside the channel before you trade. Many times, the price will immediately return inside the channel and the extra caution is worth the confirmation.

Volume Analysis And Price Action

Volume analysis is a very powerful tool in trading. Volume analysis determines the number of times a crypto asset has been traded for a certain period. It measures how many units are sold or bought within a specific time-frame. Traders use this tool as the key metric in determining the asset liquidity level.

The tool also enables traders to know how easy it is to enter and exit the market. If well utilized, traders and investors can maximize profits as well as reduce the risks involved.

If the assets have a higher volume, then it will be easy to trade both a large number or smaller quantity of assets since there several traders available.

False Volume on Exchanges

Unfortunately, the volume can be falsely indicated inside a cryptocurrency exchange. Since the exchange is its own ecosystem, some exchanges report more volume than is actually occuring. They do this for publicity since an exchange with a lot of volume would be better at matching buyers and sellers and attract more traders.

You could look at the cryptocurrency blockchain to determine the number of actual transactions. This still does not capture the actual interest because the people buying and selling are doing so on the exchanges. The exchange only needs to "settle" the transactions with the blockchain if it needs more liquidity. It is helpful to look at the charts for several exchanges and compare the volume.

Buying and Selling Volume

Volume determines the strength of price trends and warns investors about the weakness of price movements. Buyers need increased asset volume to push the prices higher.

If there is an increase in the price but a reduced number of units, then there is a lack of market interest that is likely to lead to a price reversal.

On the other hand, if the price doesn't change but large volumes that don't affect price are have occurred, this is called churn. At some point, the buyers and sellers will be exhausted and the price will likely remain steady.

Large volumes of assets traded may result in price declines or gains if the buyers and sellers are not evenly matched. This indicates a major fundamental change in the market.

Let's go back to the Supply and Demand graph. When prices rise, this is because buyers are controlling the price movement. More buyers in the market push the prices higher resulting in increased buyer volume.

The volume of each crypto asset is shown at the bottom of the price chart. The real-time charts show the trading volume in the form of vertical bar graphs at the bottom, with each bar representing the number of units exchanged for a specific period.

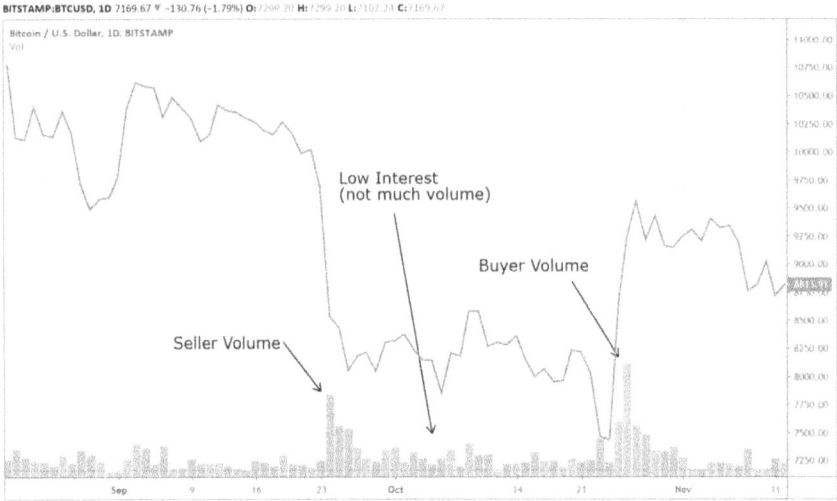

BITSTAMP:BTCUSD, 1D 7169.67 ▼ −130.76 (−1.79%) O: 7200.20 H: 7299.20 L: 7102.24 C: 7169.67

Bitcoin / U.S. Dollar, 1D, BITSTAMP

Volume bars are either red or green. A red bar indicates that the prices of the asset decreased for a specific time frame. It also indicates a selling volume in the market.

If the volume bars are green, it is an indication that prices increased during that time frame, resulting in increased buying volume.

Chapter Summary

Trend analysis is a powerful tool that provides a visual chart to help analyze cryptocurrencies and get real-time data about asset performance in the world market.

Trend lines are used to show the support and resistance levels in the price trends. Traders use trading channels to determine the entry and exit points in the market.

VOLUME INFORMATION IS USEFUL FOR DETERMINING HOW EXCITED THE MARKET IS.

CHAPTER 5
Technical Analysis Patterns

Intro

Technical analysts use price patterns to predict price movement and forecast future price movements.

Some traders have tied these patterns to human psychology. For instance, the Fear of Missing Out (FOMO) may drive many people to buy Bitcoin without really understanding why Bitcoin is a good investment. These same people are likely to spook easily and sell when the tide turns.

Learning technical analysis patterns can provide the edge in your trading.

Continuation Patterns

Continuation patterns or signals indicate that the price trend will continue in the same direction after a temporary pause. They show a higher probability of price continuity during a specific time. This can happen during an uptrend or downtrend.

All patterns should be used with another indicator for confirming the price trend.

Patterns typically occur on longer timeframes such as daily or weekly charts.

All patterns should be used with another indicator for confirming the price trend.

Cup With Handle

A cup and handle pattern is a technical indicator that forms a U-shape with a handle to complete a downward price drift. To trade using this pattern, you have to wait for the handle to either form sideways or assume a descending channel.

You should make buying decisions when the price breaks out above the top of the channel. If the price breaks away from the handle, then the pattern is completed.

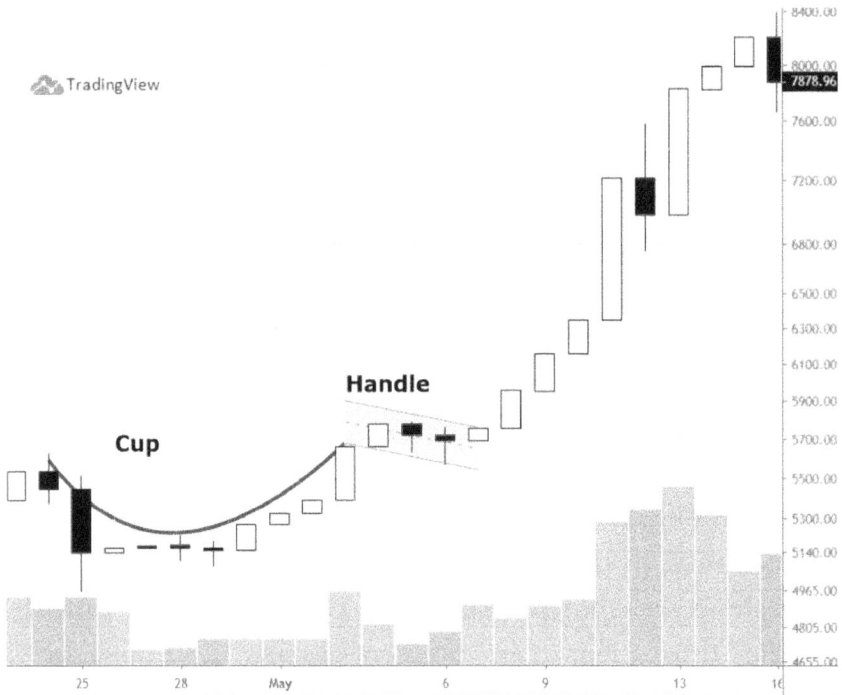

This type of pattern is a bullish continuation pattern that indicates buying opportunities. Pay particular attention to the volume - it should follow the pattern of the price in the cup. To protect the position, place a stop-loss order below the handle or below the cup depending on how volatile the price is.

Always look for a U-shaped cup because this indicates a smooth consolidation pattern. The buyers are slowly overcoming the sellers. A V-shaped cup pattern indicates too much volatility low liquidity.

Flag

A flag is a price pattern that looks like a flag on a pole. The pole is formed as a result of a sudden price increase. The flag portion of the pattern occurs when the price trends sideways.

The flag pattern takes either a bullish form with strong uptrend prices or a bearish form with downward trends. In a flag pattern, there is the likelihood of continuation from the previous price trend at the point in which the price had drifted against the same trend.

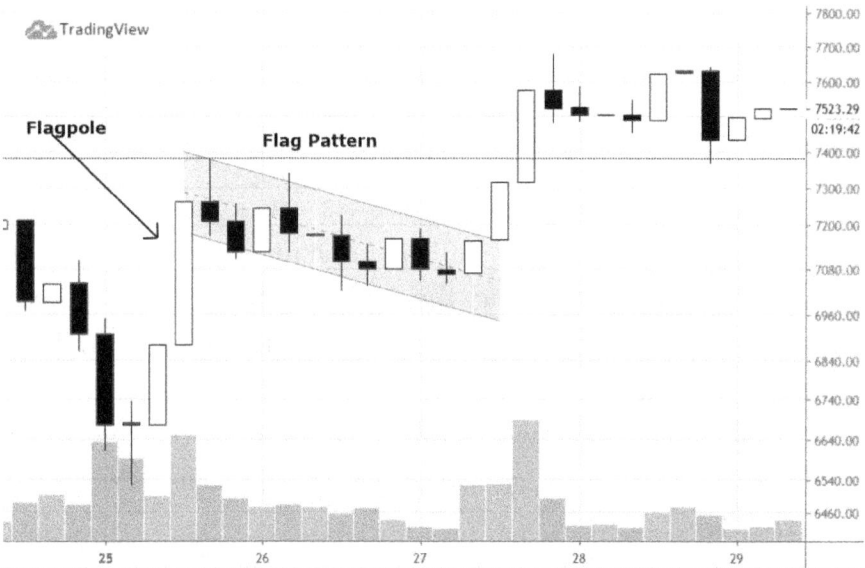

A price breakout from the flag will result in higher highs. The flag is drawn using two trend lines parallel to each other.

These lines can slope upward, sideways, or downward.

Pennant

A pennant pattern is a continuation pattern similar to the flag pattern. The difference between the two is that pennants are formed through the consolidation of trend lines to form a triangle. A large movement of trends creates the price pattern. Both bear and bullish pennant patterns use the same principle as flag patterns.

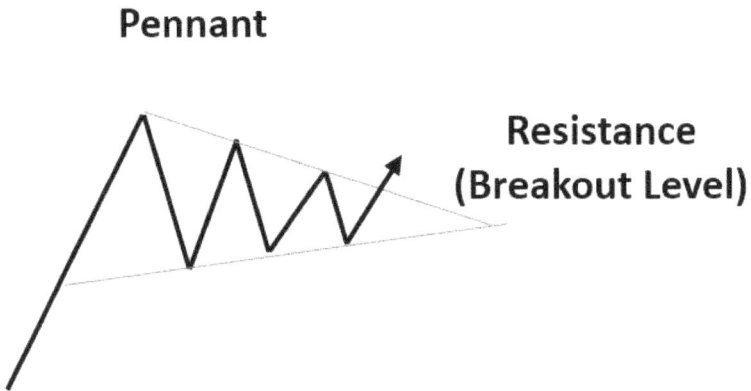

Pennant

In a bullish pennant, the trend lines are joined to form a symmetrical triangle. The bullish pennant marks a pause in the price movement along the upward trend. This allows investors to enter into long-term trades and continue making profits as prices rise. When entering a bullish trade, place a stop-loss slightly below the lower trend line to protect the trade and a profit target at the desired point above the breakout level.

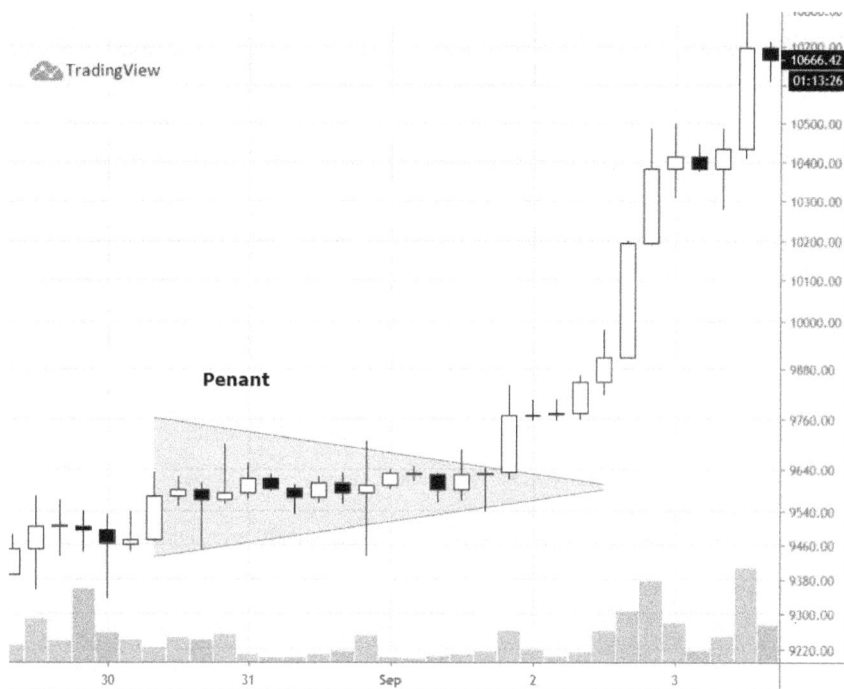

A bearish pennant indicates a pause in the price movement on a downtrend. This can occur after a sharp drop in the market price, thus forming a triangle flag. A bearish pennant gives you the opportunity to short-term trade and obtain profits from a big price fall.

Reversal Patterns

Reversal signals and patterns are used when the price pattern signals a change in the price direction. They indicate the end of an existing trend along with the turning point of the trend direction.

Reverse patterns show price changes during both the bull and bear markets. The current price pattern can pause and then continue in a new direction for a particular time frame. The price changes can be due to external constraints in the market.

For example, an uptrend as a result of taking advantage of the bull market can pause for a while. Continuous pressure in the market then facilitates the emergence of a bear market, resulting in downward price trends.

If the reversal appears at the top of the market, more investors will sell their assets than purchase additional ones, leading to a distribution pattern.

If reversal happens at the bottom of the market, it will create an accumulation pattern in which investors tend to buy more assets rather than sell existing ones.

A word of advice, wait until the pattern completes before committing to a trade.

Head & Shoulders

Head and shoulders is one commonly recognized reversal pattern. The pattern occurs at the top of the market trend and indicates a downtrend may soon occur. Head and shoulders is recognized by a series of 3 patterns: left shoulder, head, and right shoulder. Note that in the diagram below the support level (neckline) is shown as level but support may also be tilted slightly down.

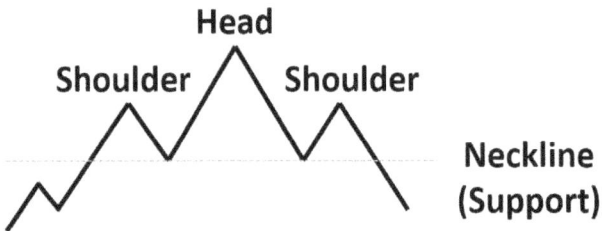

Left shoulder prices are pushed upward, resulting in shorter but higher highs before the prices retreat. That is, the left shoulder indicates that eager buyers are continuing to push prices higher before they are exhausted and sellers take over to form a trough.

During the Head phase, people are still bullish and prices surpass previous highs. When sellers take over, the price retreats to a support level.

Notice how the low at the end of the head is not trending higher. This pattern shows that the higher lows have been broken and the head's low is at or lower than the previous low from the left shoulder.

In the right shoulder, the buyers push prices higher, but the prices do not go to higher highs before breaking through the support level (confirmation line) resulting in a bearish reversal.

A return to or break below the confirmation line indicates lower lows in the price trend. The head and shoulder pattern signals, with a high degree of accuracy, that an uptrend is coming to an end.

Inverse Head & Shoulders

The inverse head pattern shoulders is a technical indicator that shows when a downtrend is about to change direction (or reverse) to an uptrend. This is the opposite of the head and shoulders pattern.

In this pattern, the price trend has three consecutive lows. The head and two shoulder elements indicate reversals in a downward trend. The left and right shoulder each have a shallow slope, and the head has the lowest trough of the three.

The presence of a bear market on the left shoulder pushes prices downward leading to new lows. The start of the bull market, on the other hand, will push the prices slightly higher.

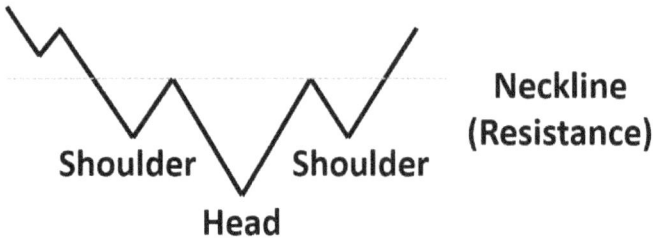

Neckline (Resistance)
Shoulder Shoulder
Head

The increasing prices do not last long before they are pushed back lower than before as a result of the bear market's return. Buyers are beginning to enter the market and absorb all the selling pressure during this period.

At the right shoulder, the prices are pushed down again but a bear market cannot push them further down. At this point, the buyers are taking a decisive stand and the prices are pushed higher and they overcome the resistance breaking through the neckline.

Double Top

The double top pattern is formed after the price of crypto assets reaches two equal highs consecutively. The pattern will look like an M. This pattern should be used on longer time-frames such as a daily chart.

This is very similar to the head and shoulders pattern but it doesn't have the additional shoulder for confirmation. Always use another indicator for confirmation with this pattern.

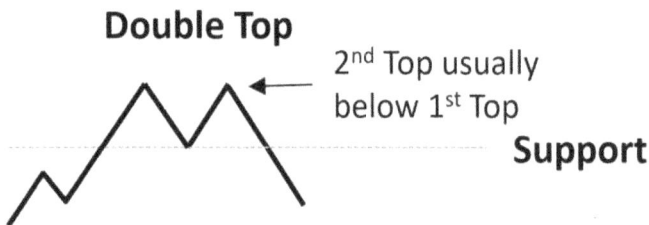

Double Top

2nd Top usually below 1st Top

Support

The double top usually occurs after an extended period of the bullish market. The 2nd top is usually slightly lower than the first top. The double top needs to break down through support to be a valid signal.

This chart pattern is very easy to misinterpret so always confirm this pattern with another indicator.

Double Bottom

This pattern is the opposite of the double top. The double bottom pattern is formed after the price of crypto assets reaches two equal lows consecutively. The pattern will look like a W. This pattern should be used on longer time-frames such as a daily chart.

Double Bottom

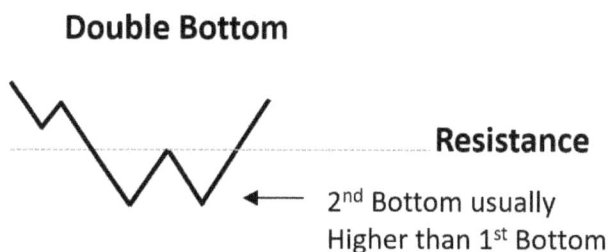

Resistance

←— 2nd Bottom usually Higher than 1st Bottom

The 2nd bottom is usually slightly higher than the first bottom. The double bottom needs to break upward through resistance to be valid.

This chart pattern is very easy to misinterpret so always confirm this pattern with another indicator.

Chapter Summary

Pattern recognition is an important technical analysis tool used by investors to determine price signals. Traders use price continuation and reversal patterns to anticipate when a price will continue or change direction.

The continuation pattern shows the potential selling opportunities, and market entry occurs after a breakout into the support level. The continuation charts used include flags, pennant, and cup with handle patterns.

The reverse pattern is used to show changes in price direction and indicates the end of an existing price trend. It is an indicator of when traders should make buying decisions. Some of the reversal patterns used include head and shoulders, reverse head and shoulders, double top, and double-bottom patterns.

Congratulations, you are wading into the exciting areas of understanding charts.

Again, thank you for purchasing this book - **Cryptocurrency Trading**.

I hope that it is answering your questions about when to buy and sell cryptocurrencies and adding to the quality to your everyday life. If so, it would be really nice if you could share this book with your friends and family by posting to <u>Facebook</u> *and* <u>Twitter</u>.

If you are enjoying this book and finding some benefit in reading this, I'd like to hear from you and hope that you could take some time to post a review on Amazon. Your feedback and support will help this author to greatly improve his writing craft for future projects and make this book even better.

You can follow this link to [<u>https://www.Amazon.com/gp/customer-reviews/write-a-review.html?asin=B084DZS6TG</u>] *now.*

I want you, the reader, to know that your review is very important and so, if you'd like to **leave a review***, all you have to do is click* <u>here</u> *and away you go.*

Thank you!

Troy

CHAPTER 6
Trend Indicators

Intro

Trend indicators are another technical analysis tool that provide information about price and asset volume to traders. Traders use trend indicators to predict where the price will likely be in the future.

Trend indicators show the direction in which the current market is moving. The price trend is likely to oscillate between high or low values in a wave-like manner.

Lagging Indicator

Lagging indicators determine price trends as well as changes in these price trends. It shows the change in price direction after a shift in the price of the asset. Traders use lagging indicators to determine Bitcoin trends and then use buy and sell signals to make investment decisions.

Lagging indicators use past prices to show where the price is trending. This type of indicator only confirms long-term trends but it does not predict them.

The lagging indicator will confirm that any long-term price shift in the market has occurred and is not a false signal. It is useful for seeing where the price has been and how the current price is acting.

Moving Averages (MA)

A moving average is a mathematical calculation for determining price trends. It is based on past prices and filters out noise from price fluctuations to determine the actual price trend.

The moving average is a lagging indicator since it is based on past asset prices.

The moving average determines the price direction for a specified period and can also show the support and resistance levels.

Traders use simple moving averages (SMA) to determine the average price for the crypto asset in a certain period. To evaluate recent asset prices, they use exponential moving averages (EMA).

Simple Moving Average (SMA)

SMA determines the arithmetic mean of an asset over a specified number of time periods.

$$SMA = \frac{A1 + A2 + A3 + \cdots + An}{n}$$

Where A_i indicates the average price in period I and n indicates the number of time periods.

Common SMA are 50, 100 and 200-day moving averages. Swing traders like to use the 50 day SMA for determining when to buy and sell. If the price is above the 50 day SMA, they assume a bull market and vice-versa if the price is below the 50 day SMA.

Exponential Moving Average (EMA)

An EMA gives more importance to recent prices and less importance to older prices. This means the EMA will follow the trend faster than a Simple Moving Average (SMA).

$$EMA = (Price[today] * WM) + (EMA[yesterday] * (1 - WM))$$

Where WM is the Weighted Multiplier which is calculated as

$$WM = \frac{2}{(selected\ time\ period + 1)}$$

And the selected time period is how long the average is calculated (ie. 10 day EMA will be 10)

EMA determines the price movement based on recent price trends. Calculate the current EMA using the previous EMA and the smoothing factor (weighted mean).

If you have a 30-day moving average, then the Weighted Multiplier will be [2/(1+30)]=0.0645

Moving Average Observations

Any moving average lags behind the actual price based on the period. The greater the period, the higher the degree of lag. For example, a 100-day MA will have a higher lag than a 10-day MA since it has prices for the last 100 days.

Trading objectives also determine the length of the moving average. For short trading intervals such as day trading, traders typically choose a short moving average, whereas, for a long-term trade, they use a long moving average.

If you have a rising moving average, it indicates an uptrend on the asset prices while a declining moving average is an indication of a downtrend.

Technical traders use moving average indicators to determine when to place buy and sell orders. The moving average can also utilize crossovers to indicate buy and sell signals. A crossover is a point of intersection in the price chart that measures the performance of the financial security and predicts future price changes.

For example, plotting a 100-day and 50-day moving average on a single chart can indicate the buy signal point when the 50-day line crosses above the 100-day line. A sell signal is indicated when the 50-day moving average line drops below the 100-day average line.

If a short-term MA trend crosses above the long-term MA, it forms a bullish crossover shown by upward momentum. If the short-term MA trend crosses below the long-term MA, it forms a bearish crossover indicated by downward momentum. You may have heard of the bearish cross with a more colorful name such as the death cross (sell signal).

How to Use Moving Averages

The easiest way to use a moving average is to determine the trend. If the price trend of the asset stays above the moving average, then it signals an uptrend. If the price trend stays below the moving average, it is an indication of a downtrend.

Experienced traders rely on EMA to ensure they are on the right track in the trading market and can filter out trades that give false signals. EMA provides earlier trade signals than SMA but can also give you false or premature signals. Therefore, observe the trend to ensure it is moving in the right direction.

EMA gives you price signals as soon as the price changes direction, while SMA moves a bit slower and is more favorable when used for long-term trades.

You can also use the moving average to filter price directions. For example, when using 200 and 50-day moving averages, you enter into a short trade when the 50-day moving average crosses the 200-day mark and a long trade when a 50-day moving average crosses above the 200-day moving average.

The crossovers will help traders analyze the price movement and make the right buying or selling decisions.

A moving average will also help in determining support and resistance levels.

Moving Average Convergence Divergence (MACD)

The Moving Average Convergence Divergence (MACD) is a great indicator that evaluates the relationship between two types of moving averages. This type of indicator consists of a chart and two lines of moving averages - a slow-moving average line (MA-slow) and a fast-moving average line (MA-fast).

If the MACD returns a positive value, and the short-term average line is above the long-term average line, then it indicates uptrend momentum. If the short-term average line is below the long-term average line, then it is an indication of downward momentum.

Always monitor the price movement. If the movement is positively oriented, then it is the right time to make purchasing decisions. If the price crosses below zero, it will be a signal to sell assets and gain profits.

Crossover lines also determine the buy and sell signals. If the fast-MA line crosses above the slow-MA line, it indicates a buy signal. If the fast-MA line crosses below the slow-MA line, it indicates a sell signal.

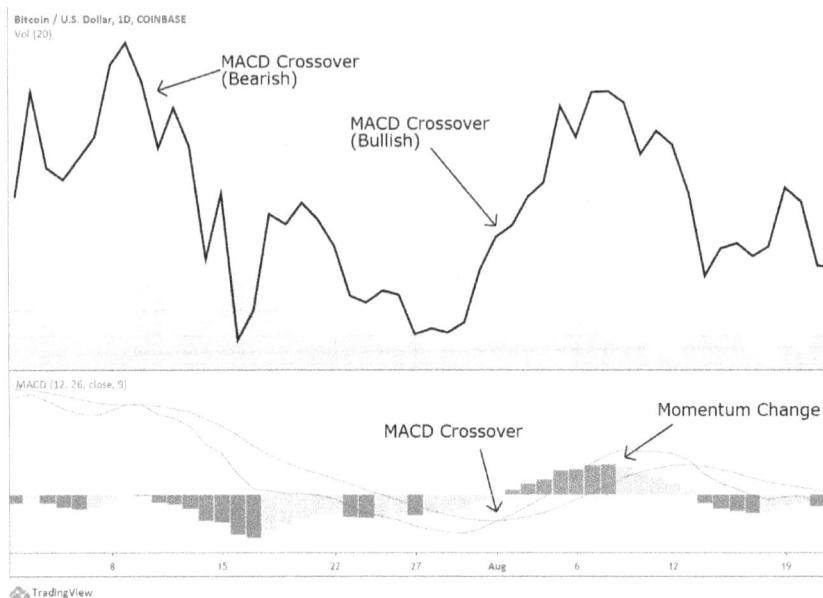

Bitcoin / U.S. Dollar, 1D, COINBASE
Vol (20)

MACD Crossover
(Bearish)

MACD Crossover
(Bullish)

MACD (12, 26, close, 9)

Momentum Change

MACD Crossover

TradingView

The histogram chart indicates the difference between the fast- and slow-moving average lines and can indicate momentum. When plotted on the chart, the lines occasionally cross over. If the difference between the fast and slow lines decreases, they approach each other and converge. But if the difference between them is large, the two lines diverge.

When the lines cross each other, they converge to indicate a reverse in price trend before starting to diverge again.

Bollinger Bands

Bollinger Bands® is another technical indicator that indicates whether a crypto asset is overbought or oversold. It uses two bands placed in standard deviation to the simple moving average line. You can pick the standard deviation. A value of 1 standard deviation means that 68% of the time, the price will remain within the two bands. For a standard deviation of 2, 95% of the time, the price will remain within the two bands.

You can see that adjusting the standard deviation lets you tune how often the price will bounce outside the lines.

Bollinger bands act as volatility indicators and are used for trading in ranging and trending markets. In a ranging market, the prices bounce from one side of the band to the other side before returning to the moving average line.

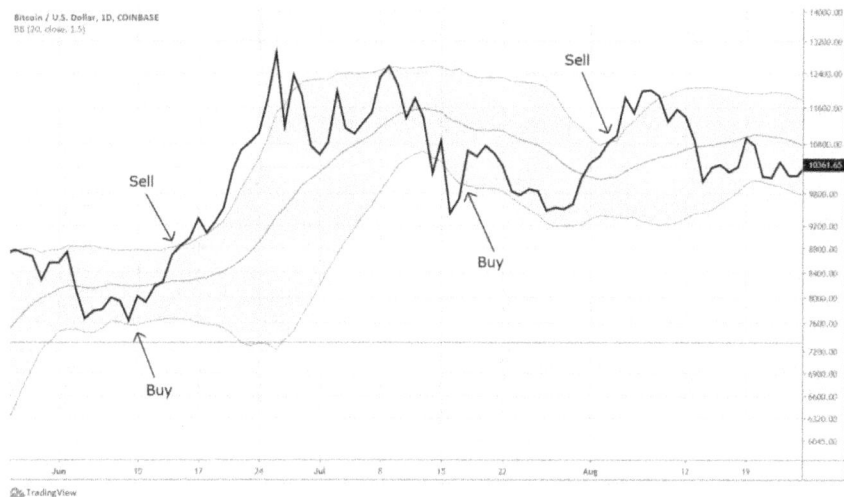

The bands represent the support and resistance levels. If the price moves towards the upper band in the chart, it is an indication that the asset is overbought. If the asset price move below the lower band then the asset is oversold.

When the price reaches either band, price tends to revert toward the average line. The chart above shows the result if you buy when the bottom band is crossed and sell when the top band is crossed.

You can use the Bollinger squeeze method to determine the entry point. If the bands approach each other (squeeze), it indicates that a breakout up or down is about to occur. The Bollinger squeeze does not indicate the price direction. Therefore, be cautious because the prices may still move in any direction.

Bollinger Bands® shouldn't be used without a confirming signal such as MACD or RSI.

Chapter Summary

In this chapter, you learned how to use trend indicators to predict when to buy and sell crypto. Some common trend indicators used include moving average, moving average convergence and divergence, and Bollinger Bands.

When using moving average indicators, you can at times use the exponential moving average (EMA), which is faster than the simple moving average (SMA). Be careful when using EMA because it can give you false signals. Confirm buying decisions if the line breaks above the moving average line and selling decisions if the break occurs below the moving average line.

> **MOVING AVERAGE CONVERGENCE AND DIVERGENCE INDICATORS GIVE YOU MORE ACCURATE SIGNALS. THE CROSSOVER-FAST AND SLOW LINES INDICATE THE TIME OF ENTRY AND EXIT FROM THE MARKET AND SHOW YOU WHETHER YOU SHOULD PLACE A SHORT OR LONG TRADE.**

CHAPTER 7
Oscillators

Intro

An oscillator is a technical indicator tool that determines whether an asset is overbought or oversold. It is widely used and helps predict the strength and momentum of the price trend as well as determine entrance and exit points in the market.

The indicator oscillates between the upper and the lower boundary lines and can respond to peaks and troughs in the trend market. An oscillator chart is plotted as either a histogram or a line graph. The trend lines in the line chart move either above or below the centerline. In banded oscillators, on the other hand, the trend lines move between the plotted bands. Banded oscillators are used to indicate price highs.

These types of indicators do well in a ranging market since they indicate when financial securities are overbought or oversold.

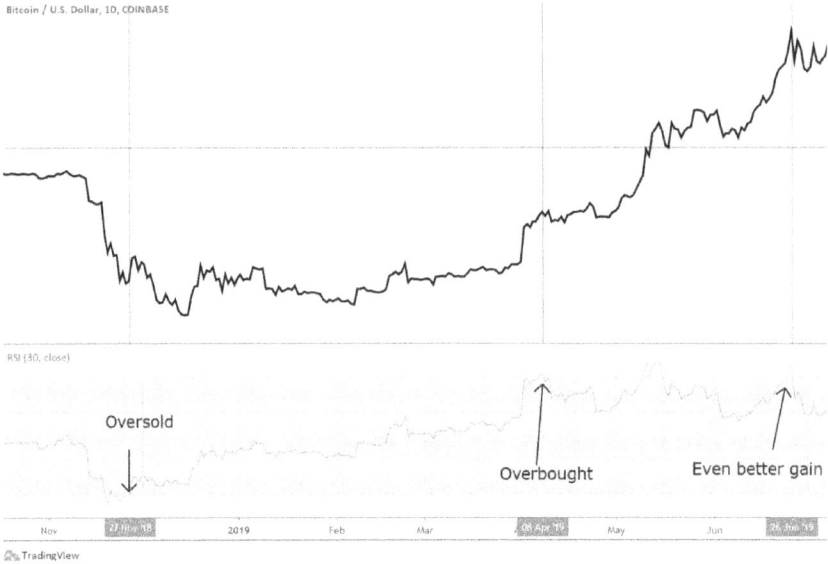

Bitcoin / U.S. Dollar, 1D, COINBASE

RSI (30, close)

Oversold

Overbought

Even better gain

TradingView

If there is not a strong directional trend, then an oscillator is useful because it indicates the type of financial security running out of steam. When the buying volume reduces over a consecutive number of days, traders will start to sell. If investors sell assets in large volumes, then the price goes down and the market is considered oversold.

When the price trend has higher highs or higher lows, it is an indication that the assets are overbought and oversold. If an oscillator with a strong trend records extreme readings for a long period, it is inadvisable to sell. It is better to ride the trend until it is exhausted.

Divergence Oscillators

If the market trend records high prices but the oscillator doesn't record higher prices, then there is a bearish divergence. Conversely, a bull divergence is formed when the oscillator records higher highs but the price is still showing lower highs.

Divergence oscillators warn traders that the current trend is nearing the end of its run.

Look at the divergence between the price and the RSI. The price is still ramping up while the oscillator is ramping down. The rest of the RSI somewhat follows the price but at the top, you can see a divergence which would have been a warning to sell.

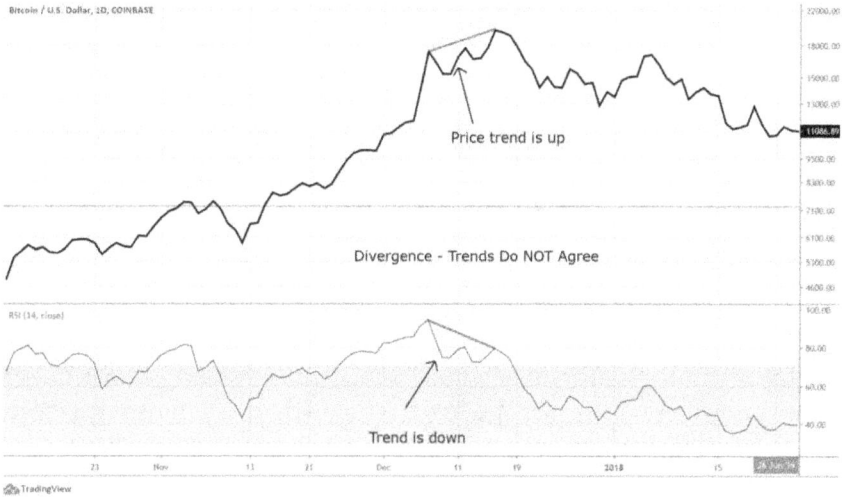

Draw the trends of the oscillator and compare it to the actual price trend to see if they agree.

Types of Oscillators

Momentum Oscillator

A momentum oscillator is used to show the rise and fall of prices compared to the actual price level. The momentum measures the rate of change in asset price.

Momentum = Today's price - price 'x' days ago

Rate of change = Today's price / price 'x' days ago

The speed, or rate, of the momentum reaches its maximum value when new investors enter the market or when a particular asset price is at its peak.

The results of the momentum oscillator can either be positive or negative. Price can be categorized as rising, flat, or falling.

- A rising price occurs when today's price records higher values than it did 'x' days ago.

- A flat price occurs when today's price increases or decreases with the same rate that it did 'x' days ago.

- A falling price occurs when today's price records lower values than it did 'x' days ago.

Relative Strength Index (RSI)

RSI is an oscillator indicator that shows price movements between zero and 100. It analyzes the gains and losses in previous prices and compares them with the current price to assess whether the values are fair.

$$RSI = 100 - \left[\frac{100}{1 + \dfrac{Average\ Gain}{Average\ Loss}} \right]$$

To interpret RSI, you have to read the price trends as overbought, which is represented by a range from 70 to 100. When the indicator is below 30, the prices are oversold.

In an uptrend movement, the asset price can move beyond 70 for a certain period before starting a downward trend. The downtrend can move to 30 and below in a long-time frame.

The overbought and oversold levels are not guarantees of accurate signals on price trends. Traders can place buy orders once the oversold trend condition is up or make short trades when the overbought condition is on a downward trend.

In RSI, buy signals are indicated by price movements below 50 that then move back above 50 again. This results in a pullback of the price trend. If RSI prices move above 50 and then move back below the 50 level, make a short trade.

Extreme RSI signals show higher tops and bottoms. As a result, the market trends will show overbought very early and record a long oversold condition.

RSI Divergence

Another RSI divergence indicator uses 2 different RSIs overlaid on each other. In the chart below, we use a fast 5 period RSI and a slower 14 period RSI. The fast RSI crossing up over the slower RSI indicates a buy. Crossing down over the slow RSI indicates a sell. The result was a $1265 gain ($5192 - $3927).

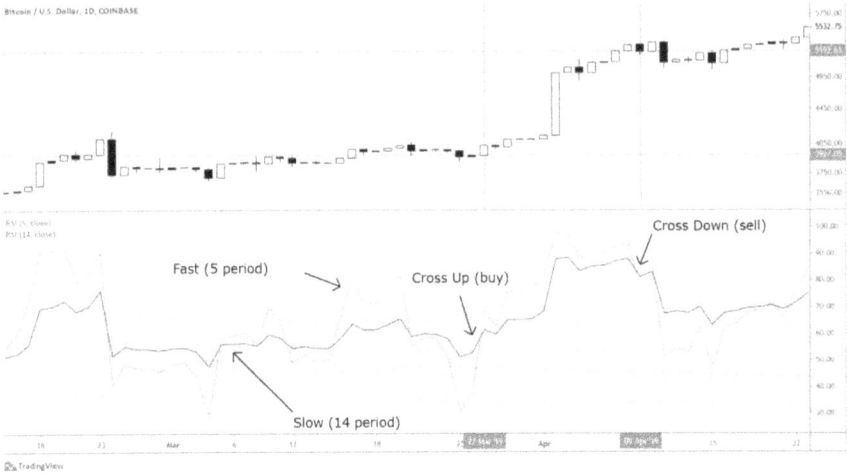

RSI Trend Lines

RSI confirms trend lines. If the RSI level is above 50, the market has an uptrend. If the RSI level is below 50, the market is in a downtrend.

If you wait for the confirmation of the trend and make the right decision, you may miss the right opportunity to take price actions. This results in less profit. The risk an investor takes based on the trendlines will determine the amount of profit gain.

In a downtrend, the RSI level will touch the 50% mark rather than the 70% to signal a bearish price momentum. Traders use horizontal trend lines in a strong trend indicated by a 30% or 70% RSI level to determine trade signals. Using both bullish and bearish price momentum of the cryptocurrency will help eliminate any false alarms generated by an RSI indicator.

Bullish and Bearish Divergence

An RSI divergence is an indication that price trends aren't

matching the RSI trend. Be alert when this happens. When the prices are rising or flat and the RSI is dropping, this is a bearish divergence and indicate prices may reverse into a downward trend.

On the other hand, if the prices are dropping or flat and the RSI is increasing, this is a bullish divergence and indicates the prices may reverse into an upward trend.

The chart at the beginning of this chapter shows a divergence between RSI and the price trend.

Divergence should act as an indication that something doesn't match up and further investigation using other indicators is needed.

Why RSI Is Often Used With MACD

MACD shows the moving average relationship between the prices of two cryptocurrency assets, while RSI measures changes in price based on the previous price highs and lows. The trend lines plotted on a MACD chart determines buy and sell signals. That is, traders only make buy orders when MACD crosses above the signal. If it crosses below the trendline, they make sell orders instead.

RSI indicates an overbought or oversold market based on the previous market price. Traders can calculate the average gains and losses in the market for a specific period.

Both RSI and MACD are often used to provide accurate information on market trends. Both indicators measure price momentum and changes in price direction.

Stochastic indicator

The stochastic indicator is a momentum indicator. It is

typically used to determine if and when an asset is overbought or oversold.

The equation for the stochastic indicator is:

$$\%K = \left(\frac{C - L14}{H14 - L14}\right) * 100$$

Where:

C = The most recent closing price

L14 = Lowest price from the last 14 trading sessions

H14 = Highest price from the last 14 trading sessions

%K = The current stochastic value

This type of indicator compares the price of the asset with its price range over a specific period.

It plots slow and fast lines. Using the plotted chart, traders can pick an entry point into the market to trade. If the stochastic level is above 80, then the assets are overbought and a downward trend is likely to occur. If the stochastic level is below 20, then the assets are oversold.

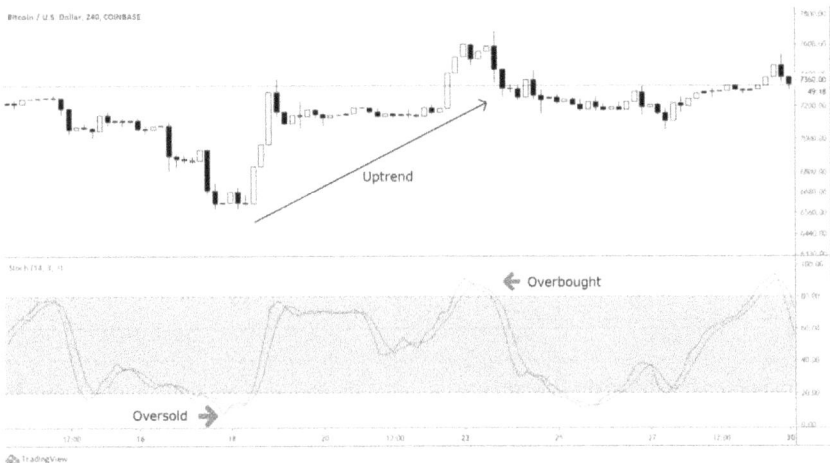

When the stochastic line is below 20, then the assets are oversold, and the chart will have an uptrend.

Difference Between Stochastic Oscillator and RSI

Both RSI and stochastic indicators predict market trends and the price momentum of a cryptocurrency. While they have the same objective, there are some key differences between the two.

A stochastic oscillator operates on the assumption that the cryptocurrency closing price should trend in the same direction as the current price trend.

RSI, on the other hand, analyzes the market trend to determine whether it is overbought or oversold using price movement momentum.

RSI determines the speed or rate of price movement for a user-specified time frame, while stochastic oscillators work best when measuring consistent price ranges.

RSI determines price movement in a trending market, while stochastic oscillators are more useful in sideways and choppy markets.

Sideways and Choppy Market

When prices shift up and down either for a short time or for an extended time period, they form a choppy market. This type of market is characterized by volatile price periods, making it difficult for traders to rely on the trend for trading.

In a sideways market, the prices of cryptocurrency assets remain in a small range. The prices don't move to higher highs; neither do they break out above the previously recorded high price.

Choppy markets are represented with rectangle chart patterns (price ranges). They occur when market participants hesitate to take action - when buyers are waiting for sellers to take any action and vice versa. Think of this as a balance between buyers and sellers.

If the trending market has an uptrend, then it will have a series of higher highs and higher lows. If the uptrends are in a choppy market, then it will be accompanied by a series of lows making a lower price shift low and a higher price shift high.

Choppy and sideways markets occur at any time, ranging from a one-minute chart to daily, weekly or monthly ones.

In sideways markets, few market factors can encourage buyers and sellers to act as they both wait for a catalyst to initiate change.

William %R

William %R is another technical indicator that determines whether cryptocurrency assets are overbought or oversold. The indicator also provides buy and sell signals to traders so they can make the right trading decisions.

The indicator operates at a price level between 0 to 100. To compare price values, the indicator value must be between 20 and 80. In the chart below, the buy occurs when the price rises across the 20 line and the sell occurs when the price drops across the 80 line.

As you can see above, this doesn't flawlessly. You'd need to set limits to get out of the trade if it doesn't trend upward. Also, you would want to confirm the buy with another indicator.

If the indicator is below the oversold line (under the minimum threshold of 20), you can make buying orders after it rises and crosses over the line.

If the indicator is above the overbought level (over the maximum value of 80), a trader can make sell orders once the indicator crosses below the line.

The overbought level indicates that the price is near the highs of the previous price range whereas the oversold level indicates that the price is below the lower end of the previous price range.

$$Williams\ \%R = \left(\frac{Highest\ High - Close}{Highest\ High - Lowest\ Low}\right)$$

Where:

Highest High = Highest price in the last X days

Close = Most recent closing price

Lowest Low = Lowest price in the last X days

Where X is typically 14 days

William % R compares the current market price with the highest price recorded in the last 14 days. An overbought signal is used to confirm an uptrend. Monitor price movement daily to note a strong upward trend that pushes prices past the previous highs.

Difference Between William %R and Stochastic

Williams %R evaluates the market trend based on recent closing prices with the highest highs for a specified time frame, while stochastic indicators evaluate the recent closing price based on lower lows.

Another difference relates to how the two indicators are scaled. Williams %R scaling uses upside-down scaling compared to the stochastic indicator.

The Williams %R is so similar to the stochastic oscillator that one or the other should be used and they should not be used to confirm each other.

Chapter Summary

Oscillators are useful tools in determining market trends and evaluating whether cryptocurrency assets are overbought or oversold. RSI, in particular, can determine the rates of price change.

You also learned about momentum oscillators, which record the speed and rate of change of the asset price. This chapter also discussed RSI divergence, how to determine and interpret RSI trendlines, and oscillators' relations to bullish and bearish divergence.

RSI INDICATORS HELP DETERMINE TRENDING MARKETS WHILE STOCHASTIC INDICATORS ARE USEFUL WHEN EVALUATING SIDEWAYS AND CHOPPY MARKETS.

CHAPTER 8
Japanese Candlesticks

Japanese Candlesticks

Japanese candlesticks influence the emotions of traders. The candlesticks represent price movement and are shown in different colors. Traders rely on these candlesticks to analyze price patterns and to forecast short-term price directions to make the right trading decisions.

Candlesticks are important when trading because they show so much information. They indicate the price points as being either open, close, high, or low within a specified time-frame by the trader.

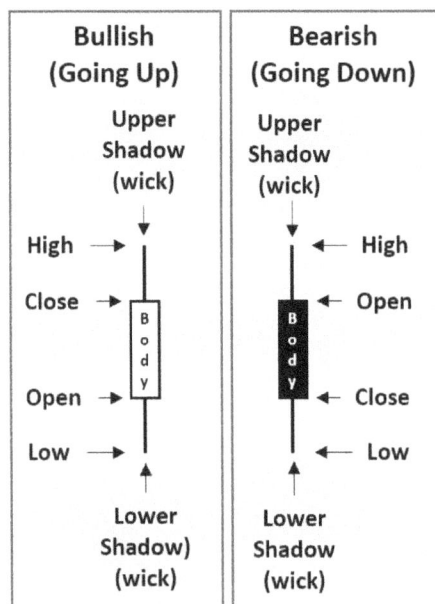

Bullish (Going Up)	Bearish (Going Down)
Upper Shadow (wick)	Upper Shadow (wick)
High →	← High
Close →	← Open
B o d y	B o d y
Open →	← Close
Low →	← Low
Lower Shadow) (wick)	Lower Shadow (wick)

The candlestick shows important data including the opening price, the high and low, and the closing price for the time period. The candlestick body size graphically shows the difference between the opening and closing price.

The candles can be used within any time-frame to show the price action in that span. On a 1 hour chart, the time period is 1 hour. On a daily chart, the time period encompasses a day so the body will probably be much larger than in the hourly chart.

The body shows the range of prices between the opening and closing of the time period. If the body is black, then the closing price is lower than the opening price. In other words, there was a downtrend in that time-frame. If the body is empty (white), then the closing had a higher price value than the opening price and the market had an uptrend. The candles can also be customized to display a red or green color for downtrends and uptrends respectively.

The upper and lower wicks are sometimes called shadows and indicate the high and low prices during the time period. The wicks are an important part of the chart because they indicate the entire range of prices. Traders use the shadows of candlesticks to anticipate investor sentiment and will be the focus of this chapter.

Candlestick Patterns

A candlestick contains an amazing amount of information in a small space. Although the price movement appears random, sometimes it forms patterns useful in analyzing a trade.

The candlestick wicks or shadows indicate how high or low a price went before the close. If the closing price was near the high or low, the wicks will be small or may not exist at all. Large wicks indicate the price rose or fell significantly but then returned closer to the opening price. A large wick means the buyers or sellers could not keep the momentum going and may indicate exhaustion.

Advantages of Japanese Candlesticks

A. Simple and easy-to-analyze system

• Candlestick charts are more powerful than bar and line graphs. They have a simple and easy-to-analyze interface that helps you get detailed information about the market instantaneously. You can easily determine the state of the cryptocurrency market at a glance.

• By looking at the color of the candlestick's real body, you can know whether the market is bullish or bearish.

• Traders use candlesticks to interpret the supply and demand of crypto assets in the market. Investors can easily analyze the market trend and identify the critical factors leading to trend reversals to make price action decisions. This can also serve as an early warning to the investors.

B. Quickly identify price direction

• Looking at the color of the candlestick's chart, traders can quickly determine price movement or direction. It can confirm if an uptrend price direction is a bullish momentum or if the market is having a bearish momentum.

C. Quickly identify market patterns

• Candlestick charts are useful in displaying bullish and bearish market patterns that cannot be created by other methods. Each candlestick displays currency ranges with both open, close, high, and low elements.

D. Facilitate decision-making

• Candlestick bar charts show the price movement between the opening and closing times. With this information, traders can make the right buying and selling decisions.

E. Validate Other Indicators and Methods

• Candlesticks are combined with other technical indicators to provide investors with reliable information use to determine entry and exit points.

Candlesticks, in conjunction with other indicators, can determine trend reversal points and price breakouts points in the market and help traders create effective trading strategies.

Types of Japanese candlesticks

Spinning tops

Spinning tops are candlesticks that have a small body with long upper and lower wicks. This candlestick pattern shows indecisive actions in both buyers and sellers.

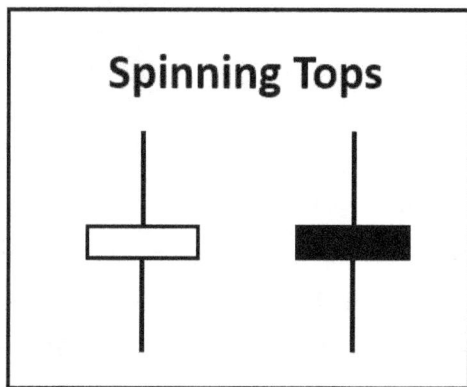

The small body indicates that there is little price movement between the opening and closing time-frames. The long wicks indicate a struggle between the buyers and sellers and suggest that neither has gained an upper hand, resulting in a standoff market.

If spinning tops occur during a market uptrend, then only a few buyers are in the market. This will likely lead to a change in price direction.

Likewise, if spinning tops occur during a market downtrend, there are few sellers currently in the market, and changes

in price direction are likely to occur.

Marubozu

Marubozu is another type of Japanese candlestick. The candle has no shadows, indicating its high and low values are the same as the open and close price values.

The candle bodies can be filled or hollow and they indicate a bearish or bullish market.

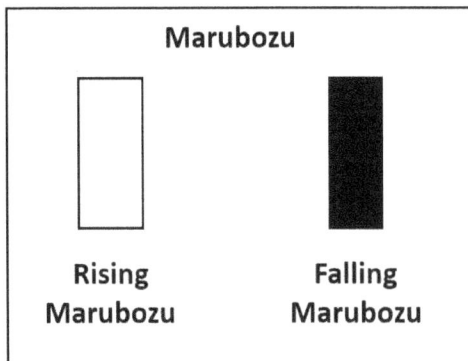

Marubozu

Rising Marubozu **Falling Marubozu**

A hollow or white Marubozu body has no wick showing that the opening price was also the low price for the time period. Similarly, its closing price is equal to the time-frame's high price. This candlestick reveals a bullish market in which the buyers in the market have control during the entire trading period.

Alternatively, the black Marubozu, or the filled body, does not have shadows either, showing that the opening price is also the session high while its closing price is the same as the session low price. The black Marubozu is a bearish candle since sellers have more control over price during the trading period.

Doji

A Doji is created when the candlestick has the same opening and closing price but moves up and down during the session. The price on the upper and lower shadows may vary. Doji indicates an indecisive market.

Due to the indecisive actions of buyers and sellers in the market, neither can gain control of the market.

The price of the cryptocurrency can move either above or below the opening value during a trading period before closing near to the opening price.

The candlestick has a small real body with upper and lower shadows and is sometimes described as a plus sign, a cross, and an inverted cross.

Long White Candle Followed By Doji

A Doji created after a long white Marubozu body is a pattern demonstrating that the buyers are exhausted and becoming very weak.

If the price has to maintain an upward trend, then more buyers are required. Unfortunately, there are none, and instead, more sellers enter the market to push the price back down.

Long Black Candle Followed By Doji

In a situation where the Doji is created through a black Marubozu body with a series of candlesticks, then it indicates that sellers are exhausted and becoming weak.

For the price to continue on a downward trend, more sellers have to enter into the market. Due to the cheap prices of the cryptocurrency, more buyers are willing to get into the market.

Hammer and Hanging Man

The Hammer and Hanging Man candlesticks have a short body and a long wick below the body. The long wick indicates there was a lot of activity against where it closed during the period. The short body indicates the price closed after reversing the momentum.

In both the Hammer and the Hanging Man, the close can be above or below the open. In other words, either can be black or white (or red or green if using colors). The main characteristic is that the tail below the body should be at least 2 times the body size. The larger the tail compared to the body, the better the signal.

The difference between the hammer and hanging man is where they appear. The hammer occurs during a downtrend while the hanging man occurs during an uptrend.

For both the hammer and hanging man, there may be a short upper wick or no wick.

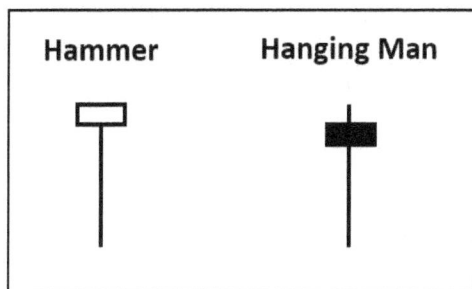

Hammer   Hanging Man

Hammer

A hammer forms during a downward trend and it represents a bullish reversal pattern. The hammer indicates that the price opened and decreased fairly radically before reversing and closing higher. The buyers were able to overcome the sellers.

Having a lower long shadow is an indication that the sellers aggressively pushed the prices lower, but the buyers over-rode that momentum and took control of prices.

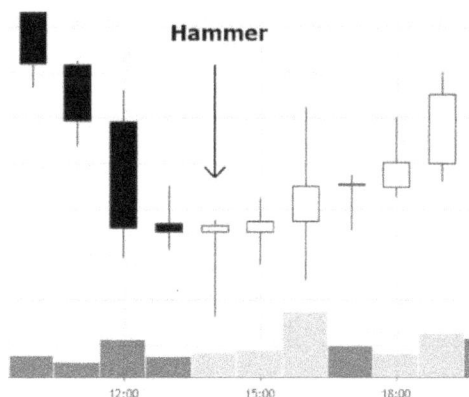

Hammer

If the hammer is on a downward trend instead of a sideways trend, watch the following candles for confirmation before placing buy orders.

Note that volume should be similar to the previous volume to be valid. False hammers are created when the volume is much lower than previous candles.

Hanging Man

A hanging man looks almost identical to the hammer. This price pattern occurs during an uptrend and it indicates the buyers are losing momentum.

In this case, buyers opened strong and tried to push the price up, but met resistance from sellers who pushed the price back below the opening value. This is an indication that not enough buyers were available to keep up with the momentum of the rising price.

Similarly to the hammer, the volume of the hanging man should be similar to the previous volumes to be valid. False hanging men are created when the volume is much lower than previous candles.

Inverted Hammer and Shooting Star

These two types of candlesticks look almost the same. The only difference between the two is whether you are operating on a downward trend or an uptrend.

Both inverted hammer and shooting star candlesticks have a

small body, a long upper shadow, and either no lower shadow or a very short lower shadow. The length of the upper shadow should be at least 2 times the height of the body. The longer the upper shadow is, the more convincing the signal.

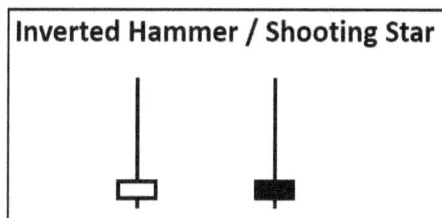

A bullish reversal candlestick represents an inverted hammer, while a bearish reversal candlestick signal represents a shooting star.

Inverted Hammer

An inverted hammer is drawn on a downward trend. The dropping price in the market is an indication of potential price reversals. Its long upper shadow is an indication of increased buy orders from the buyers as they try to push prices higher. However, the sellers ultimately take control of the market and push the price back down.

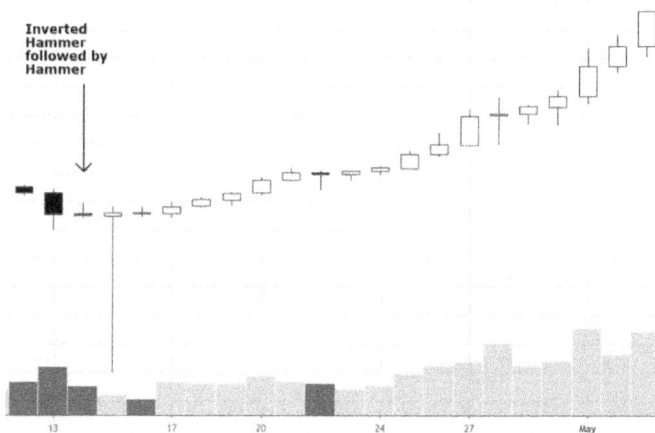

Shooting Star

A shooting star resembles a bearish reversal pattern that occurs in an uptrend direction. The presence of a shooting star is an indication that the price closed near the opening price. That is, buyers tried to push the prices up but were overpowered by sellers who pushed the price back to the bottom.

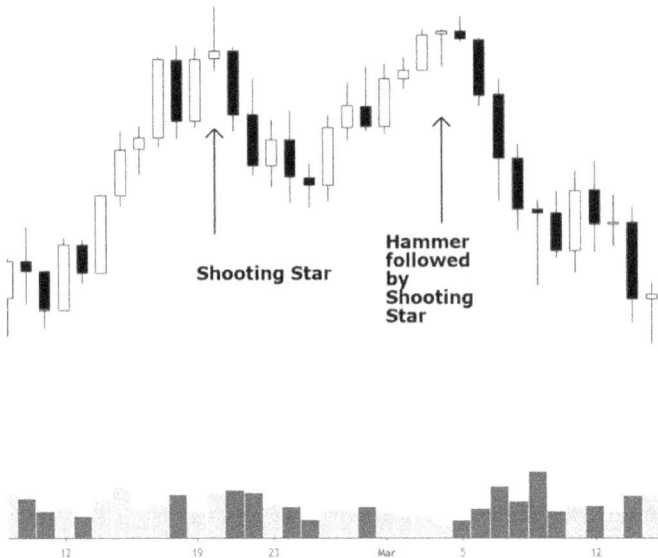

Candlestick Patterns

Candlesticks patterns are useful tools for determining price action as well as price momentum.

As you would expect, the candlestick patterns are time-sensitive. The chart patterns are limited based on the review rate whether daily, weekly, or monthly. The potency of the charts reduces rapidly once the pattern has been completed.

These patterns can either be reversal or continuation patterns. A reversal pattern is one where there is a shift in the price direction while a continuation pattern is one that forecasts an extended continuation of the current price direction.

Bull and Bear Engulfing

The bullish engulfing pattern is made up of 2 candlesticks which means it is not as accurate as a 3 candlestick pattern. It is used to predict a bear trend reversal. The first candlestick is down but the following candlestick is larger and in the opposite direction (engulfs the first candlestick).

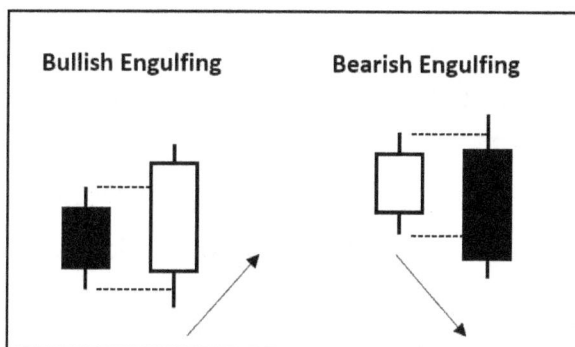

The idea behind this pattern is that the bulls completely overpowered the bears in the previous pattern. The larger the bull candlestick is compared to the bear candlestick, the stronger the signal.

The bearish engulfing pattern is simply the opposite and may indicate a bearish trend reversal.

Two candle patterns are not great at predicting short term patterns so use these with a longer time-frame chart such as 4 hour or daily charts.

Evening and Morning Star

The evening star is a bullish reversal pattern that occurs in an upward trend. The reversal has a large white candle followed by a spinning top (can be either white or black) followed by a black candle down that is at least 1/2 the size of the large white candle.

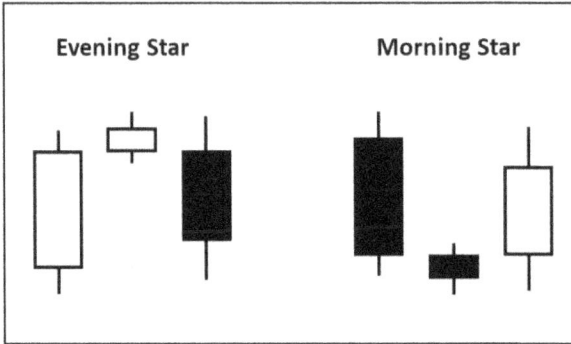

The morning star is the opposite and signals the reversal of a bearish trend.

An example of a morning star is shown below. The first morning star had an RSI confirmation which would increase the trader's confidence in the trade.

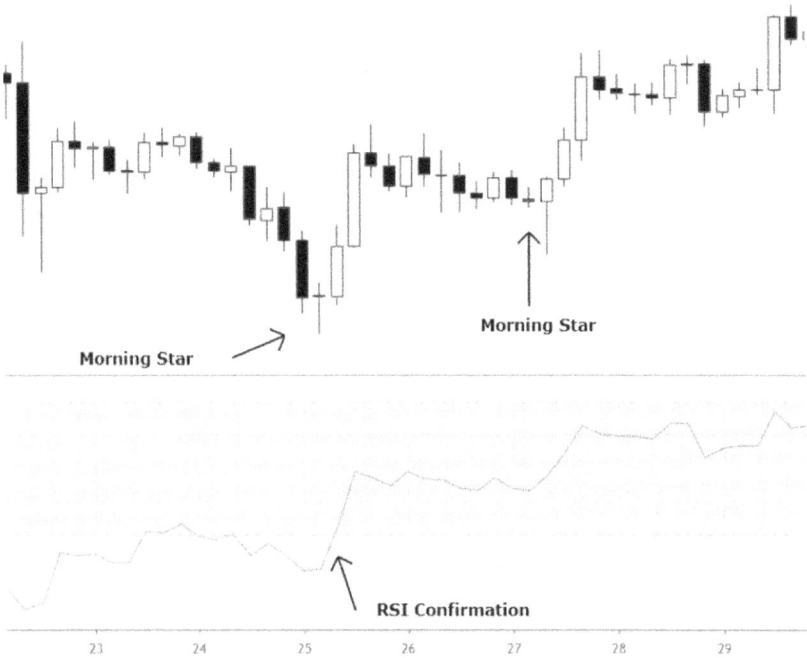

Chapter Summary

The candlestick is very important in trade analysis. It helps you see how control shifts among key market players. Careful analysis of the candlestick charts will enable you to make the right price action decisions.

The candle bar charts highlight buy and sell signals, and investors can quickly make trading decisions just by glancing at them. Because the bars are easy to create and read, traders quickly identify price direction with them.

THERE ARE DIFFERENT TYPES OF CANDLESTICKS TRADERS CAN USE TO MONITOR PRICE MOVEMENT AND DETERMINE THE ENTRY AND EXIT POINTS. CANDLE BAR PATTERNS ALSO FORECAST FUTURE PRICE CHANGES.

CHAPTER 9
Automated Trading

Automated Trading

Automated trade is a programmed computing system that allows traders to establish certain trade rules for entry and exit into the market. Once these rules are met, the computing systems execute the set instructions.

Traders can add specific entry and exit points into the system and let the system monitor the trades. Once the entries match the set criteria, trades are placed automatically.

Traders can create the entry and exit points using any of the criteria discussed in the preceding sections.

There are different types of automated trading software on the web, and traders can choose one and customize it to meet their trading needs.

Trading Bots

A trading bot is a program created to do repetitive tasks. The program is set based on specific parameters or rules, making them a faster way to trade. The bots monitor price movements and analyze market trends in terms of trade volumes, trading orders, price, and time. It makes trading decisions based on the analyzed information and preprogrammed rules.

Due to the increased market volatility, trading bots have become more popular in the crypto market. Traders are using bots to control their cryptocurrency investment 24/7, even when they're away.

Setting the bots correctly with clearly specified entry and exit points will enable trades to be automatically executed, and they're more effective compared to observing and setting trades manually.

Bitcoin traders trade passively and spend the majority of their time analyzing the trading market. Therefore, trading bots will help them be more effective as traders don't have to constantly watch the market.

When using bots, you must be very careful to avoid phishing attacks. There are phishing bots designed to specifically steal personal data from the web like your account details.

When looking for a trading bot, choose the one that's free from coding errors and has minimal downtime. Look at the user's feedback before investing in a particular bot.

Top Trading Bots

Cryptohopper

This is a popular trading bot that includes a paper trading option. It simplifies trading processes and helps users increase profit margins. This type of trading bot runs on the cloud and offers 24/7 services to users.

The platform has an interactive user interface, which only requires the user to log in to its dashboard before starting to trade. Once you buy the trading bot, it only requires five minutes to set up to be ready to start trading.

Cryptohopper offers advanced trading tools to make it easy for traders to use. Next to the dashboard is an embedded external signaler, which allows new subscribers to join other trading analysis lists online.

It uses machine learning to determine market prices and trading volumes, then sends signals directly to users' bots. The bots make automatic buy and sell orders on behalf of the users after receiving the signals.

This type of bot allows users to take advantage of the bull market and set stop-loss limits when entering a trade. Users rely on the dashboard to monitor price trends and trades made. It also uses technical analysis tools like RSI, MACD, and Bollinger Bands.

3Commas

3Commas is another reputable trading bot in the market. It provides web-based services to users so they can trade 24/7.

When you buy this trading bot, you can monitor trading activities on your dashboard from any device. The bot allows you to set stop-loss limits to maximize your profits and minimize your losses.

This web-based platform has a crypto portfolio feature, which enables you to not only create and analyze trades but also to back-test a crypto portfolio.

MetaTrader

MetaTrader is an automated trading platform that is popular among stock and forex traders. MetaTrader is a little different than the other trading bots listed here because it requires a separate broker to do the trades.

Traders must choose a reputable broker to link MetaTrader to. Be very careful choosing a broker because there are many scam brokers.

Because of its stock market and forex history, MetaTrader has a rich library of functions to analyze charts to generate trading signals. The platform provides advanced technical analysis, expert advice, and an automated trading system.

You can install the application on your computer or your mobile device and enjoy its benefits.

MetaTrader4 and MetaTrader5 are customizable based on user preferences. After downloading the free application (MetaTrader makes its money from the brokers it connects to), a user can define the market conditions based on predetermined factors and set stop-loss limits and profit targets. Once the conditions are met, the trading bot can place buy and sell orders. Investors with an Android device can additionally install the MetaTrader app and monitor their trade at any time.

DIY Python Programming

The Python coding language has become a preferred choice for algorithmic trading developers since it has free library packages for commercial use. Automated trading developers rely on its open-source scientific library including packages like Pandas, PyAlgoTrade, NumPy, Pybacktest to produce statistical data.

Python trading programs are popular and many free examples are available to traders. Only experienced traders who know how to program should jump into using Python for trading. However, once familiar with the trading essentials, these programs allow the trader to customize their algorithms.

Customizing all the trading criteria is the main feature of DIY

Python programs. It is easy to write the code and evaluate algorithmic trading structures due to its functional programming approach. Python is a high-level programming language, which means you only need to enter a few lines of code for the instructions to execute instead of writing instructions out in detail.

FreqTrade

FreqTrade is a cryptocurrency trading bot built using the Python language. This trading bot requires that you have basic knowledge of the Python programming language to run any trading patterns.

You also have to learn how trading works and know the amount of profits or losses you expect to incur if you use FreqTrade as your trading tool. You can read through various analysis before you commit money. You can use the dry-run to practice paper trading with the bot before investing real money.

With the FreqTrade platform, you can use features like back-testing, which provides you with a simulated environment to test buy and sell signals based on historical data. The platform also provides edge position sizing where traders can calculate their win rate, determine risk/reward ratio, enter stop-loss points, and adjust the position size.

Access Trading Bots Via Mobile Device

You can build and run a trading bot through your mobile device. You can also back-test or run automated trading strategies in the cloud using mobile-based apps. The apps allow you to create your trading strategy based on predefined parameters. You can also monitor and control the trades using your mobile device.

The apps are easy to use and community-driven, so traders can trade and interact with other like-minded individuals in the platform forums.

You don't have to be an expert in programming since no coding skills are needed for automated trading. You can test the automated trading strategies in the cloud through your mobile device.

You will have total control of your trading account. All you need is to build your strategy on your mobile app the test your strategy with real market conditions. Constantly monitor and control your trading strategies using your mobile device.

You can also turn the alert feature on. Set alerts to receive Bitcoin news via your mobile device. This can through an SMS text to your phone or email.

Advantages of Automated Trading

• Speed of execution: Since automated trading systems are designed beforehand, they can execute instructions automatically. They can scan and execute multiple market conditions at a fast rate compared to manual analysis.

• Accuracy of information: Automated trading is a computer programmed platform that executes trades based on given parameters. The parameters or predefined conditions entered into the system are double-checked for any errors before execution. This ensures data accuracy and the use of trade signals to complete a transaction. Double-checking eliminates errors made by humans on manual entries to the system.

• Removes human emotions: Automated trading systems eliminate human emotion while trading because traders are constrained within particular predefined criteria. This avoids irrational decisions made by humans based on their emotions.

• Backtesting: Automated trading systems allow traders to analyze trading patterns to know what works and does not work for them based on their past data. If past data worked for them, there is a possibility that the new data and algorithms will work for them. Looking at past data also allows traders to tune their algorithms to eliminate any flaws that can affect their current trading activities.

• Reduce transaction cost: In automated trading, you don't have to spend a lot of time monitoring the trading market. Repetitive transactions are done without any constant supervision of the markets, which reduces the costs of monitoring the market and transaction costs.

Cryptocurrency Exchanges

Cryptocurrency exchanges are web-based platforms designed to allow traders to buy and sell cryptocurrencies using fiat money.

It is ironic that even though Bitcoin was designed as a decentralized currency, the ecosystem has evolved into using centralized exchanges for exchanging fiat money for cryptocurrencies.

Cryptocurrency Exchange Policies

Payment merchants and crypto exchange companies have to

comply with established banking regulations to operate as a financial company in the United States and Europe.

These exchange firms are required by the government agencies to monitor internal policies and procedures and control any illegal activity. Exchanges are required to pay close attention to AML and KYC procedures.

KYC (Know Your Customer)

KYC is a requirement for financial institutions to identify and verify customers. Exchanges monitor whether clients are using the exchanges for money laundering operations. Typically this requires proving your identity by submitting an ID or passport when opening an account on the exchange.

If you only buy and sell cryptocurrency without using an exchange, you may not run into KYC barriers. If you trade outside centralized exchanges, you don't have to declare your identity either.

Although KYC tools are mostly used by centralized organizations, cryptocurrency exchange firms apply KYC in their decentralized ecosystem. Many people assume that Bitcoin is anonymous but as a result of KYC, it really isn't. The transaction is recorded forever in the Bitcoin blockchain. Although the Bitcoin transaction doesn't require anyone to disclose their identity when performing a transaction, if the coin eventually is sent to a crypto exchange, the government will be able to subpoena the identity of the person who received the Bitcoin and then trace it backward. Think of unraveling the transaction history as pulling a thread on a sweater.

AML (Anti-Money Laundering)

Anti-money laundering laws and regulations were created to control the exchange of illegal money. AML laws are expansive and cover tax evasion, corruption or abuse of public money, and market manipulation via the use of wash-trading techniques among others.

The exchange firms must comply with AML regulations. The firms should monitor all transactions and report any suspicious accounts to AML. Cryptocurrency exchange firms and other companies use KYC software tools to detect any fraudulent activity and also to verify customer identity and viability.

AML and KYC are used interchangeably in the cryptocurrency market, and they're both associated with identifying and accepting clients, monitoring transactions, and handling risk management.

Automated Trading with Exchanges

There are ways to exchange one crypto coin for another without going through an exchange and the associated KYC or AML but that is outside the scope of this book.

Bitcoin traders use Bitcoin exchange platforms to exchange fiat currency and altcoins. Exchanges act as the intermediary between the buyers and the sellers.

The cryptocurrency exchange publishes an Application Program Interface (API) to allow bots to connect to them. The bot uses the API to connect to the cryptocurrency exchange to buy and sell cryptocurrency.

Automated transactions through an exchange platform have

to register with the exchange to be verified and authenticated to access the system. Once the verification is complete, your account is opened. After establishing an account, you can transfer funds to your account and begin buying and selling crypto coins.

Conversion fees

Depositing or withdrawing money to your account typically results in a transaction fee by the exchange. The fee charged depends on the payment option used. Bank transfers are usually cheaper than credit card purchase fees.

Bitcoin exchanges also attract transaction fees which are applied when you make buy and sell orders within the exchange platform. The fee depends on the volume of your transactio1n.

Hacking of Bitcoin Exchanges

Although almost all Bitcoin exchange platforms have safeguards for crypto asset security, it is not a guarantee against threats on the exchange ecosystem. In the past, hackers have been able to make their way through exchange platforms like Mt. Gox and Binance where they stole customer's cryptocurrency.

The cryptocurrency itself is very secure, but exchange platforms concentrate a lot of cryptocurrency in one place and thus are a profitable target for hackers.

When the exchange platform experiences a major hack, users tend to be affected. Some exchanges have insurance for all or part of your account.

Chapter Summary

Automated systems are an essential tool in the financial

market. They run programs to monitor and analyze market trends and determine buy and sell signals.

Users don't have to manually monitor the market trends and trade volumes before making trading decisions.

Users use trading bot automated systems to effectively monitor the market and provide trading alerts to users. These trading bots ensure the users interact with the market and maximize their investment.

Trading bots are not for everyone. If you buy and hold Bitcoin for a predefined time, then trading bots will not work for you. There are different types of trading bots you can use. With Bitcoin, popular bots include Cryptohopper, 3Commas, and MetaTrader. Other trading bots like FreqTrade require manual configuration and manual tuning but then provide automated monitoring of market trends.

Automated trading systems are integrated with the top Bitcoin exchange platforms to make it easy to exchange currency from fiat money to Bitcoins and back. There are different exchange platforms and each platform charges different fees and provides different services.

Exchanges are required by law to comply with AML and KYC rules and regulations and ensure they offer higher protection to their customers.

Whew! You made it through! Are you as excited about the possibilities of cryptocurrency trading as I am?

What Did You Think of Cryptocurrency Trading: Beginners Guide to Buying and Selling Bitcoin and other Cryptocurrencies?

Thank you for purchasing this book **Cryptocurrency Trading**. *I know you could have picked any number of books to read, but you picked this book and for that I am extremely grateful.*

I hope that it added at value and quality to your everyday life. If so, it would be really nice if you could share this book with your friends and family by posting to <u>Facebook</u> *and* <u>Twitter</u>.

If you enjoyed this book and found some benefit in reading this, I'd like to hear from you and hope that you could take some time to post a review on Amazon. Your feedback and support will help this author to greatly improve his writing craft for future projects and make this book even better.

You can follow this link to [<u>https://www.Amazon.com/gp/customer-reviews/write-a-review.html?asin=B084DZS6TG</u>] now.

I want you, the reader, to know that your review is very important and so, if you'd like to **leave a review**, *all you have to do is click* <u>here</u> *and away you go.*

I wish you all the best in your future cryptocurrency trading!

Thank you!

Troy